CREATURES GREAT AND SMALL

CREATURES
GREAT AND SMALL

by
CHERRY EVANS

HODDER AND STOUGHTON

PRINTED IN GREAT BRITAIN FOR HODDER
AND STOUGHTON LIMITED, ST. PAUL'S HOUSE,
WARWICK LANE, LONDON, E.C.4 BY C. TINLING
AND CO. LIMITED, LIVERPOOL, LONDON AND
PRESCOT

To My Husband
who loves all our creatures great and small
only a little more than they love him

ILLUSTRATIONS

* Photographs by Mr. Alec C. Cowper, of Perth

Chapter 1

ONCE we lived in London, in a respectable animal-free way. We had a golden red dachshund called Kirsche, who was mine, and a beautiful blue fawn whippet called Rheidol who was my husband's. Apart from the pigeons opposite, whose acquaintance we made in a casual way, and who were in any case too busy courting to pay much attention to us, we had no other close animal friends.

But we came to Scotland, and moved into a small semi-derelict grey stone farmhouse which clung to the slopes of the Sidlaw Hills. There was an orchard of old apple trees, gnarled and lichen covered, surrounding the house, and a six-foot-high forest of nettles which grew close to the walls and peered and nodded in the windows. Rheidol stalked importantly about inspecting her new domain, snuffling down old drainpipes for rats, and picking her way delicately through the matted undergrowth. Kirsche began to hunt in the scratchy depths of the nettles, dachshund legs moving fast over the ground, her clear high-pitched voice giving tongue as she smelt the unmistakable smell of rabbit. At night she flopped by the fire, or lay on her back, paws in the air, tummy pink and itchy from nettle stings. Rheidol lay curled in a chair, her ears half pricked, to show she was not really asleep. Her lip pouched slightly over her teeth, and we could see the glint of her eye watching us.

Our house, Kilspindie, was built with the stones of Kilspindie Castle, home of William Wallace's aunt, where he lived as a boy more than six hundred years ago. Nothing now remains of the castle except the old dovecote. The Manse, the Church, the farmhouse and the school were all built of the stones of the old castle, but even the site of it is now forgotten. On the one side

11

our garden was bordered by a large and ancient stone wall, on the other by a row of yew trees leaning and nodding into the road. A stream ran below them, disappearing in a silent cascade under the churchyard path.

"First we must divert the stream and make ponds in the garden," my husband said to me.

"First we must get rid of the nettles, and turn the garden into lawn," I said.

Neither of these things looked in the least like happening. We got three garden firms to give estimates for removing the nettles and sowing lawn grass. They all looked sadly at the immense jungle, and shook their heads.

"It would take ten years to clear that," they said, and "I doubt it could ever really be done."

In the meantime we covered the whole garden with a strong solution of sodium chlorate, and cut out the more spindly of the apple trees. Kirsche continued to hunt busily through the dingle below the church, and Rheidol came up the hill with us to hunt rabbits. She was a dog of fantastic speed and cunning. We would creep up behind a gorse bush, with Kirsche hunting and shouting low to the ground, while Rheidol waited the other side for the rabbit to be flushed. A sudden sprint from Rheidol, a murderous snap of her steel-toothed jaws, her ears spread wide, and the rabbit was dead. Below us the Carse of Gowrie stretched away towards the deep blue of the Tay, and high on the other side stood the peak of Norman Law, burial place of a long-dead Viking with his ship. The sun glowed red to the west behind us, and I could feel the sharp bite of the October frost. We picked up the rabbit and whistled the dogs to follow as we made our way down to the slim spiral of smoke rising from the chimney.

"Rabbit tea for dogs," Humphrey said to Rheidol, who walked close behind him, her nose twitching slightly.

All winter we dug and hacked at the nettle and thistle roots in that garden. The nettle roots were long and yellow, intertwined like a thick mattress, the stalks sharp and brittle standing like spears in thick array. The docks had long tap-roots which defied spade and fork, and usually broke, leaving us lying breathless on the ground.

As the nights drew in, the geese started to come down from the north on their long winter journey. They flew over our house, and we could hear them at night honking under the starlit sky. In the evening they came low over the wide reed beds of the Tay, dropping slow out of the sky, their soft grey wings folding like giant umbrellas as they wheeled ever earthwards, and at last shut their wings as their feet hit the water with a soft hiss and plop. Humphrey would sometimes go down to the reeds and shoot one in the evening, for they made good eating, but he said he could hardly bear it, they were such beautiful and romantic birds.

One evening he came back with a live goose.

"I found her lying in the reeds at Port Allan. I think she must have been wounded."

She was clearly very ill, and so thin that her breastbone stuck out like a razor as I took her in my arms. It took us a long time to learn, and I doubt if we ever really will, that if a wild bird gets below a certain level of subsistence, nothing anybody can do will bring it back. In the winter a wild bird is often so weakened by hunger and constant lack of food that it will not have enough resistance to pull through. And also however much you may care for a wild animal, however much you love it, it is still wild, and the shock of being in close proximity to a human being is often more than it can stand.

But when Humphrey brought in this goose, we did not know these things. We made a straw nest for her in our bedroom, and kept the fire on all night to warm her. The ground outside was like iron, and the stars brittle with frost. We managed to get her to eat a little bread soaked in warm milk and sherry, which we pushed inside her beak. Humphrey held it open, and I pushed the soft pellets of food inside. I think she must have been riddled with shot, besides being so thin. All night long we heard her soft goose voice, muttering to herself. Poor goose, I wondered, was she very unhappy? Did she mind the smell of human beings, the smothered feeling of a roof overhead, instead of the clear sky and the stars?

She lived with us for a week. We kept her alive all that time, feeding her on soft bread and sherry, for she was too weak to take anything else. But she was clearly getting worse.

"We must take her to the vet," Humphrey said towards the end, "although I doubt if there is anything he can do."

We got into the car, Humphrey driving, and me holding the goose in my arms. It was a clear moonlit night, the stars very bright in the frosty sky. Mr. Macrae, the vet, examined our goose.

"No," he said. "There is nothing you can do. She will die anyway. I had much better knock her on the head."

But I could not bear it, and so we carried her back with us to the car. As we drove along the road from Perth I suddenly felt the goose give a slight heave in my arms.

"Stop the car," I said to Humphrey. "I think she hears the other geese flying past."

We stopped; and I got out, with her still in my arms. Overhead dark against the moon a skein of twenty geese were flying over, in symmetrical V-formation, their necks spread wide, talking to each other in soft voices as they flew. My goose suddenly spread her neck out, and I could feel her trying to raise her wings.

"Gug-gug, kok-kok," she said softly, and as the other geese answered her flying on to the south, she went quite limp and dead in my arms.

"Oh geese flying south, high and free in the sky, take my goose with you." I prayed.

We buried her at the foot of our orchard where she could hear the wild geese flying over the apple trees, and in the spring could see them flying north again, calling in clear voices across the green morning.

.   .   .

Mr. Macrae came in one day soon afterwards on his rounds.

"I was sorry about your goose," he said. "But when you're ready for them I've got a lovely pair of Birmingham Roller pigeons, I know you'll like them."

Mr. Macrae is like that: he is just plain nice. But somehow I could not bear to have any pigeons just then; I grieved terribly for my goose.

Not long after that Humphrey brought back two more geese. Like the first one, they were greylags. One had just been tipped with shot in the wing, the other had stunned herself against a telegraph post. Both were plump and well fed, and looked as if they stood a better chance of recovery. We put them in one of those conical wooden hen houses with a wire chicken run outside, and they soon got to know us, running up to the wire and honking when we came out with food for them. Our small son Adam, who was nearly two, became very attached to them, and would run out with small pieces of raw potato, which was what they liked best of all. We fed them on wheat, and sometimes a layers' mash, but they really preferred raw potato. It was a terribly cold winter, and every morning when we went out we found their water bowl frozen solid, and had to take it in and unthaw it in the kitchen.

I liked both these geese, but I never became so attached to them as I had to the first goose of all. They were independent-minded, and used to honk in loud, rather cross voices when we came out to see them. If I made goose noises to them, they answered back, but louder and crosser, as if they considered I was someone to be driven away. The first cage we kept them in was not very satisfactory, because they kept getting their beaks caught in the wire netting and cutting them.

"We can't let them free yet," Humphrey said, "because for one thing, it's such a cold winter, and all their friends have gone south. And also they're not quite recovered enough yet to survive on their own. We'll have to make a much bigger enclosure for them, and clip their wings."

I hated the idea of this, but they both had cuts on their beaks where they rubbed them against the wire netting, and

15

they were clearly assured of a much better chance of survival if we kept them through the winter. We made a large wire netting enclosure in the field to the east of our house, through which another stream runs, and this we dammed up to make a pool, thinking that wild geese like to swim on water. This we discovered was not true, and we came to the conclusion that geese only go on water as a protection from man, dogs and other natural enemies, so that they can sleep at night secure from attack. Our geese soon became reasonably tame, and regarded us more as natural sources of food than as enemies. The dogs they disregarded. But never once in the time they lived with us did we see either of our geese go down to the pool we had so carefully made and swim on it.

That first winter was terribly cold. We put food out for the birds on the kitchen window sill, and it was always crowded. Blue tits and coal tits hung upside down on the coconut, or pecked at our strings of nuts, while blackbirds and thrushes ate everything from bread and old porridge to bacon rind.

One bitter January afternoon when Humphrey was helping with the afternoon milking he found a small frozen wagtail lying as if dead in the milking parlour. He picked her up and put her inside his jacket, and gradually with the warmth felt her beginning to stir to life. He brought her back, and that night she slept in our bedroom, perched on top of our four-poster bed. I sprinkled crumbs of bread all over the floor, and in the morning when it was light, she flew down and hopped about picking up crumbs. About eleven o'clock when the sun became really hot, she flew off out of the window.

"Silly little bird," Humphrey said. "She should have migrated long ago."

Still, after all that food and the night in the warmth, we felt that she stood a good chance of survival.

That very afternoon Humphrey was again in the milking parlour, and to his surprise noticed the same wagtail lying again as if dead on the concrete floor. She was lying in the same place and must surely have been the same bird. Again he picked her up, and revived her with heat inside his coat. She came back again, and spent the night with us in our bedroom, and after a good meal flew out in the morning.

On the third evening just as the sun was beginning to hang red and lowering in the sullen winter sky, and the rushes stand up black as spears in the long expanse of snow-covered fields, Humphrey was not surprised to see our friend the wagtail back again in the dairy. She spent her third and last night with us, and then disappeared into the blue morning sky. We never saw her again, and hoped that she had at last won her way through to some warmer climate.

. . .

One evening when we were staying with my parents, who lived about three miles south of Kilspindie, Humphrey was out flighting in the reeds. He said he would be back by eight, but the clock struck the half hour and there was no sign of him. I was already worried, because the River Tay is two miles wide here with dangerous currents. It is also covered with mud banks, and miles and miles of reeds which hiss and rustle in the wind. It was November, and very cold. Somehow I found my appetite for food had completely disappeared. Kirsche and Rheidol were sitting gazing into the fire with their backs turned, when I suddenly saw their ears prick, and Rheidol got up and went towards the door. It opened, and Humphrey stood there, dripping wet from head to foot. I have never seen anyone so wet. Apparently the coble, which is what we call the heavy flat-bottomed boats that go out in the Tay, had been drawn up on a mud bank.

"Then the tide started to go out," Humphrey explained. "And when I came to try and shift her, she was absolutely stuck, and too heavy to move down into the water. I thought you'd be worried about me if I waited for the tide to go right down, and then come in again, so I held the gun in one hand, and the dog in the other, and simply swam for the shore."

I took him quickly to have a hot bath. Spring, the spaniel,

17

B

was sitting dripping in the kitchen—a very wet dog indeed, and very glad of the hot milk and bones Humphrey had given her.

.   .   .

Gradually the cold winter wore on, until the ground softened in spring. Snowdrops appeared in our garden, and we worked more frantically than ever at clearing the nettle roots and old docks which matted it. I tore the retina of my left eye with a dry nettle stalk, and had to go into hospital for a week, which was a terrible nuisance, besides being very sore. When I came out again, spring had really hit the garden: grass and young nettles were coming up everywhere, there were primroses out in the woods, and Adam was quite pleased to see me back. The dogs went wild with delight, and even the geese came up to me calling softly and accepted some slices of raw potato from my hand.

May came, and the weather was soft and warm, the geese lay about, and made dust baths for themselves scratched out of the earth. Humphrey acquired some game hens, dark black and red and greeny ones called Black Reds, with little brown hens like pheasants, and white ones, with a cock with a huge red and white tail. They strutted about the garden, fought each other and scratched up the flower beds. At night they roosted in the laurel trees. The geese kept their distance, and the game birds were too busy fighting their own battles to interfere. I worked harder than ever in the garden, and one beautiful sunny May afternoon our daughter Charlotte was born.

She had a bright red face, all screwed up, and Adam was rather shocked when he saw her, but Humphrey and I thought she was beautiful. Kirsche knew about babies: she was already attached to Adam, and now spent her mornings lying in the sun guarding the pram. Rheidol behaved as if there were no baby in the house: she was not a dog who cared much for children.

As we sat outside the front door in the long couch grass that

18

summer, with Adam's smart London pram hock-deep in nettles, we thought how lovely it would be if this were lawn. The apple trees and pear trees became a canopy of pink and white lace, and the nettles came up stronger than ever. Three times that summer we ploughed the whole garden, picking out nettle and dock roots in the wake of the plough, and throwing them aside into heaps where we burnt them. One part only we didn't plough, and that was where a young partridge had made her nest. In spite of us, and the dogs, and the constant ploughing right in front of the house she managed to hatch out and rear four babies. Tiny brown balls of fluff they were, scuttering and running in the long grass and nettles.

This season we rented three small fields round the house, in which we planned to graze cattle.

The field north-west of the house is called the Dovecote Field. The old Kilspindie Castle dovecote stands there, solidly built of stone, rectangular in shape with a sloping slate roof, and three raised wooden gables in front where pigeons come in and out. There is a low door, and inside are stone nesting boxes tiered up to the roof. Before the eighteenth century, when there was no feeding for beasts through the winter, the majority of cattle were killed and salted down for winter feeding, and the only fresh meat was very often the pigeons picked out at night from the dovecote. The right to own a dovecote was once a considerable status symbol. Every Scottish laird had his own attached to the house, or at any rate somewhere near it. There are many of these left, all over Scotland, but very often, alas, in a bad state of repair. When we came to Kilspindie, our dovecote was falling down too, but we managed to get it patched up, and now it should last for another hundred years or so. There were only about five wild pigeons inhabiting it when we came, but the number soon rose to over forty.

The top field of all is called the Croft Field, and here are the two remaining walls of an old croft, long ruined. Below them grow a few blackcurrant bushes, and one or two apple and

19

plum trees which often yield good fruit. Now there is no one left who once lived there, who ate the plums and picked the blackcurrants. Perhaps far away over the sea there is some old old woman who remembers it as it was, with the thatch on the roof, and the scent of the mauve and white potato blossom, and the waving oats, who remembers the feel of the soft mossy turf under her bare feet as she ran up the hill to fetch the two patient precious cows. But no, I think not, it has been a ruin and unlived in for too long.

In the long summer evenings, Humphrey would pull out the ragwort in this field, watched by the five small cattle he had bought. We called them The Girls collectively, but individually Brownie, Cinnamon, Blackie, Brownie's Friend and Blackie's Friend.

Brownie was their leader—a tough but scraggy heifer the colour of home-made fudge, her forelock sticking up in a tuft in front of her head. She was always the one who pushed her way first through the sagging wires of the fence, to emerge into the road for a preliminary sniff through the farm yards, until she made up her mind and headed her small herd across the broad fields of the Carse at a fast gallop. Her Friend was black in colour, and stuck closely behind her—a cow of loyalty but little individual character.

Blackie was the second in command, much bigger than Brownie, and always, in a clumsy way, making a bid for the leadership of the herd. But she never succeeded, being worsted by the superior cunning and plain dogged courage of Brownie. Blackie's Friend was black also, and indistinguishable in appearance and character from Brownie's Friend: they were both rather dull yes-cows.

Cinnamon was differentiated by the slight curl all over her coat, which was a deep rich colour and very handsome. She was rather an aloof cow, with little interest in the constant struggle for power, tending to support whoever was actually in command. This meant of course Brownie.

Brownie and her Friends were bought at the market in

Perth as a commercial enterprise; we decided to keep them on the Dovecote and Croft fields all summer, and then sell them fattened in the autumn. It was a mistaken idea, because we got to love them all in spite of their many drawbacks. One of their drawbacks was that they would never stay confined to the fields we had put them in. They broke out, they tore through the fence, they galloped through the remains of our garden, or went foraging in the farmyard eating the winter hay and turnips, or gorging themselves on the cabbages in Mrs. Simpson's garden up the hill.

Mr. Simpson is the farm grieve, or manager; both he and his wife have scarlet hair: so do their two sons and four daughters. Tom, the son who works at Kilspindie, married Sadie who also had red hair, and both Hughie and Fiona, their children, have scarlet hair too. Fortunately Mrs. Simpson is a friend, and didn't mind Brownie in her garden as much as I should have done.

Sometimes Brownie and her friends would gallop in a mad stampede down the road, across the road which runs along the foot of the hill and into Pitroddie, the farm next door. We knew that it was becoming more and more difficult to keep Brownie, and besides we had long lost any hopes of making any profit out of her and her friends.

"It's not as if they were pedigree Aberdeen Angus, and we could sell them for thousands of pounds," Humphrey explained. "They're just ordinary cross-bred beef cattle, and I doubt now if we'll even get as much as we paid for them."

Sadly we had a final cattle round-up, and drove them into the stable at the farm where we gave them a final grooming, and an extra special meal of cowcake and oats. After dark that night, Humphrey and I slipped out with a lantern to look at them. They looked so peaceful lying there, especially Brownie, all fluffed up like a huge teddy bear.

"Humphrey," I said. "Suppose we just keep Brownie?"

We looked at each other, and back at that huge fluffy toffee-coloured heifer. Brownie stayed.

But of course it was no use; she missed her friends, and she was never in her field. We began to dread the telephone late at night, when we had just settled down for a cosy evening, or lying asleep just before dawn.

"Is that Mrs. Evans? . . . It'll be your brown heifer . . . She's in the top field at Balmyre . . . She's away over the hill at Nether Durdie . . . She's just left Myreside and is going down the main road towards North Murie . . ."

It was splendid for our figures. We got quite thin chasing up the hillside, running across the mountain, calling for Brownie. But we got very bad-tempered. And Brownie became less tame and wilder and crosser, and even a little bit savage.

"Brownie is missing her friends," Humphrey said to me one day. "She will be happier with other cows."

He had just been dragged on the end of a rope right up the plough of the Dovecote Field. Adam thought it was a splendid performance.

"Daddy's just like a cowboy," he said.

So we said goodbye to Brownie, but for several years we always used to look for fluffy dun-coloured cows standing in fields in the hope that we might see Brownie. I thought I did see her once, about two years later. It was in a field near Stirling, and I opened the car window and shouted her name as we drove past. She was a perfectly enormous dun cow, with an unusual tuft on her forehead, and she looked up at me in a speculative way as I shouted.

While we still had Brownie and her friends, in the late summer, we acquired our first hawk.

"Our goshawk is arriving tomorrow," Humphrey said casually one evening in September. It was a phrase I was later to know quite well; just then I was unprepared for such a *fait accompli*.

"But what on earth are we going to do with a goshawk?" I demanded. "How can we feed it? Won't it eat Charlotte?"

I had visions of an eagle-sized bird descending on the house, or perhaps hovering above, vulture-like, peering into the pram.

22

Humphrey explained patiently, and at some length. He had always been keen on falconry, and had often kept hawks before we lived in London. A goshawk was short-winged in any event, and didn't hover. We would feed her on beef, pigeon, starling, rabbit—whatever came to hand. "She has to have castings twice a week, like an owl, otherwise her pannel gets furred up. And her food must be raw, and as fresh as you can make it."

I was still clueless. "But what is a pannel? And what are castings?"

"The pannel is the lining of the hawk's stomach, and castings are bits of feather or fur or bone, anything which can rub round it and clean it out. When you give a hawk castings she retains these in her stomach, and then spits them out later in a neat pellet or casting—you must have seen owls' pellets lying around."

The next morning Humphrey drove to the aerodrome to fetch our goshawk. She was a passage hawk who had come from Norway, and we called her Melindwr, which is a Welsh name and means "Honeyed Waters". It was not a particularly auspicious or appropriate name for her, for she was a most scary bird, and never in our brief acquaintance were our relations with her honeyed. She was a beautiful speckled brown, with a cream and brown speckled chest, and pale honey-coloured eyes which peered savagely and unblinkingly at the torch I held in a shaking hand. We carried the case into a shed and unpacked her in the dark. I held the torch, while Humphrey slipped his hands into the case and gently eased her out. Holding her wings firmly to her sides so she should not damage any feathers, he held out her legs to me to slip on the smooth leather jesses he had prepared. These are slitted thongs which slip round a hawk's legs, one for each leg. The other ends are attached to a small brass swivel, which has a longer leash on the other end. This leash is what you hold the hawk by, or use to tie it to its perch.

Seeing those wicked curved claws thrust toward me at the end of Melindwr's long yellow legs, my fingers became all thumbs. I took the torch out of my mouth, where I was holding it for better use of my hands, and said, "I can't. I'll hold her, you do it."

Humphrey promptly put the torch in his mouth, and placed Melindwr into my hands. She was still too shocked by the sudden dark to struggle, and I felt her body, surprisingly light and feathery in my hands. Except for those wicked claws I might have been holding a large hen.

Humphrey soon had the jesses tied on to his satisfaction and twisted into a swivel, to which he attached a leash. He then put a leather hawking glove on his left fist, and holding the leash asked me to manoeuvre Melindwr on to it. She balanced there, precarious and uncertain, and when I opened the doors of the shed and let in the daylight, promptly flew off. She could not of course fly far, because of her jesses and leash, and hung screaming and flapping upside down from the fist. This is what is called in hawking language bating off. She certainly looked in a terrible bate. Humphrey put his free hand gently under her breast and put her back on again. She stood there wild and uncertain for a moment, savagery and fury in her round yellow eyes, her beak open and panting slightly. Then she bated off again.

"This is what is called manning the hawk," Humphrey explained. "It may take some days."

I saw Melindwr panting slightly, casting her wicked eyes on Humphrey before bating off again, and left them to it.

"You can give me a hand later with belling her," he said.

Having a hawk was a very time-consuming job. She took all our time, or at least all Humphrey's just at first. According to his reference books, a hawk when wild must first be waked or watched, in order to tame her sufficiently to sit on the falconer's fist without bating. This meant holding the hawk every single waking moment until eventually, overcome by sleep, she was able to extend her confidence to her master. Humphrey spent two nights awake with Melindwr, sitting in the kitchen, stroking her with a feather so as not to remove the natural protective oils from her feathers by too much contact with his hand, reading poetry to her, trying to soothe and tame her with the constant sound of his voice.

We had no electricity in those days, only an auxiliary engine, which sometimes worked and sometimes not. I cooked on rural gas, and we ran the engine for short periods while we worked the vacuum cleaner, or alternatively the electric iron, but not both together. When the engine broke down, or ran out of fuel, which it did occasionally, we lived by candlelight, and ironed with flat irons heated on an open fire. They were never the right temperature, either too cold and made black sooty marks on the clean clothes, or too hot and made warm brown scorch marks. So as not to run the engine all night, and run the risk of her seizing up, Humphrey lit a good supply of candles, set out in order on the red Formica kitchen table, and I switched out the engine and went to bed, feeling mean and unhelpful.

Kirsche and Rheidol came with me, Kirsche as usual tunnelling to the remotest corner of the bed like some small plush hot water bottle, or perhaps motivated by an atavistic memory of earlier dachshunds pursuing badgers through dark tunnelled setts. Rheidol, who was an aloof independent dog, apart from her passion for Humphrey, condescended to lie stretched out, her head on the pillow beside me. Humphrey she considered was definitely demented; what was the point of that flapping screaming bird who might or might not ultimately be able to catch rabbits, while she, Rheidol, on any crisp October day could nip through the gorse bushes, using Kirsche as flusher out, and pick up three or four rabbits in the afternoon? Rheidol's mouth opened slightly, and she showed her teeth, and curled her lip in contempt.

It was on the third day of our acquaintance with Melindwr that misadventure struck us. Melindwr was perhaps not manned, but she would at least sit on a fist without bating. It was a windy day with scraps of bright sunshine, and fluffy cumulus tearing through the sky like giant snowflakes in a wind. As he had done for the last two days, Humphrey took Melindwr in the car with him down to the Estate Office, perched on his left fist, and beginning to look sleepy and ruffled. He had had a new swivel sent to him that morning from a hawk merchant in Lahore, for he felt the one he had was too light and small for the weight of the leash.

He slipped the new swivel into his pocket meaning to change it when he got a moment. The morning wore on, Humphrey working at his desk, people coming in and out, the telephone ringing, Rheidol lying under a large black typewriter cover, peering malevolently at Melindwr, who was perched on a padded broomstick thrust between two filing cabinets, the floor beneath well strewn with newspaper to catch her mutes— which is a hawking term for hawks' messes. Melindwr stood on tiptoe, her neck on a stalk, her shoulders hunched, peering venomously back. About mid-morning there was a pause in the stream of daily activities, and Humphrey slipped on his glove, and picking up Melindwr took her out into the sunshine in the yard outside. Holding her jesses tightly in his gloved hand, he untied the leash from the swivel, and carefully pushed the ends of the jesses back through it. Then he slipped the old swivel back into his pocket and took out his new one. And at that precise moment fate struck.

My mother came into the yard accompanied by two of her greyhounds, which raced towards Humphrey and jumped up on him. He raised his left arm at once to put Melindwr out of their reach, and with the sudden movement, she jerked her jesses out of his hand and was free. She went straight into the wind, down, down, the wind whistling through her feathers, half flying, half blown past all possible perches. Humphrey ran after her, hoping to keep her in sight long enough to mark down where she was heading, so that at night he might perhaps find her in some tree where he could either climb up and catch her, or else lure her down into a trap. She was far too untrained either to come down to the fist or to the lure. But he soon became unsighted. My mother jumped into her car and rushed down the drive in the direction Melindwr had gone, Humphrey got into his car and went in a north-east parallel direction. But it was too late. There was no sign of her.

Humphrey made several traps with bownets and dead pigeons covered with wire snares to trap her feet, and waited out by them at night. She could not have been far away because we found evidence of carefully plucked pigeon's feathers; this meant that a large hawk was killing for herself somewhere in the woods. But she disdained our dead pigeon traps. Flying from tree to tree as she obviously was, she was enjoying to the full the keen pleasure of swooping from a tree on to some unsuspecting creature below, catching it, killing it and eating it warm. She must have found a roosting pigeon, for a goshawk, which is a short-wing hawk, could never catch one in free flight.

It was a disheartening end to our brief acquaintanceship. Humphrey advertised her loss in the papers, in the hopes that someone might report a sight of her or sound of her bells. He gave our telephone number, and the Office one too. But he felt this might be a forlorn hope.

All day he searched, and stayed out until dark with his traps in the hope of hearing her bell where she was roosting. There was no sign of her. Next morning the telephone started to ring. People all over Perthshire, it seemed, had seen Melindwr. Mostly it was a kestrel, or in some places in the north undoubtedly a buzzard. But some of the reports were distinctly amusing.

An engine driver telephoned us from a café in Dunkeld. "I saw a big black bird like a crow from the cab of my engine near Dalwhinnie."

It was kind of him to telephone, but what he had probably seen was either a large crow or a raven. Melindwr, with her brown back and creamy speckled front could never have been mistaken for a black bird.

Our most amusing telephone call was from a woman in Kirkcaldy. "I think I've seen your lost hawk," she said excitedly. "I just keeked out of my back window, and saw a strange bird climbing up the back of the cinema."

We assured her it wasn't Melindwr, but we couldn't think—any more than she could—what it could have been.

The response to our advertisement amazed us, and we were more than grateful to all the many kind people who telephoned and tried to help us in our search. Humphrey followed up all the more likely clues. But they proved in the end to be nothing.

"One good thing," Humphrey consoled me, "She only had her jesses on, no leash or swivel, so she won't be likely to get hung up."

We did in fact find out what had happened to her about six months later. A gamekeeper friend of ours told us that a goshawk with a bell was living in the woods at Panmure, just north of Dundee, and leading a happy poaching life among the reared pheasants. She was utterly wild, and much too canny to let us even catch a glimpse of her.

As the autumn wore on towards winter, and the leaves turned golden and dropped from the trees in a flutter of confetti, our two greylag geese began to get restless. We had clipped their wings with a pair of kitchen scissors in the early spring when we had let them out of their pen. Now their wings had grown long again. They were both healthy and well, and we felt we should put no obstacle in the way of their joining their friends and winging their way south again, once more part of a vast goose flock.

One golden October day one of the geese took off and circled round the farm buildings three times uttering glad goose cries; she had rediscovered the use of her wings. She was off to join her kith and kindred down in the river; the call of the south was strong in her; she felt the wind lift under her pinion feathers, she could sense the other geese calling her. We were forgotten, or if remembered at all, only as a summer refuge, a resting place she had stayed in, before passing on. She flew down over the ruins of the mill house, over the wide Carse of Gowrie, interspersed with trees and straggling hedges, and long deep draining streams called Pows, over the stubble, the half harvested potato shaws, over the whispering reeds to fold her wings, mushroom-curved, and drop into the river beside her fellow geese.

What must she have had to talk about all night? Gug, gug, kok, kok, one could hear them whispering through the rustling reeds.

Her friend had not realized that her wings had grown. All day she ran round and round in the field uttering despairing goose cries. The moon was full that night, and we could not bear to sleep for her sad voice, crying and crying to the moon, and to the other geese sailing southward.

"Take me with you, take me with you, don't let me die here in this cold place inhabited by men, far from the reed beds and the quacking ducks and the companionship of the great gaggle moving ever southwards from the iced beds of the north."

We went to the window, now Humphrey, now me; there was nothing we could do. We could feed our goose, we could rescue her, we could provide her with a shelter from the world, but now that she was ready to rejoin the world, we could not show her how to go back. We were powerless, helpless, and unhappy.

At dawn her cries changed; they became more cheerful, less despairing. We rushed to the window, and saw her taking a long steady run across the rough grass of the field, her wings raised and flapping slowly to catch the wind. Then she soared upwards and winged over the grey lands of dawn to join her friend. She had remembered how to fly.

Chapter 2

In December Humphrey had a letter from Bill Ruttledge, a hawking friend of his, offering us his half-trained Norwegian goshawk, Sven. He sent off a telegram the same day. About a week later Sven arrived at Perth Station in an enormous packing case, complete with a curious contraption rather like a fencing mask. Bill had worn this to protect his face; in a covering letter he warned Humphrey that she was inclined to be moody, and strike out with a claw. For Sven was not a male goshawk as we had supposed, but a large female. We changed her name to Svenna.

We converted the stable, formerly a garage, into a mews, and Humphrey balanced a large branch across the wall at the back from which he suspended a piece of sacking with weights sewn into the bottom. This was so that if Svenna bated off while sitting on the branch with her leash tied round it, she would be able to stick her talons into the sacking and claw her way back to an upright position. If this is not done, and the hawk is alone, she may hang upside down for hours until she finally dies. This is what, alas, very often happens to hawks who escape with leash and swivel, and why it is so vital to recapture them.

We eyed the fencing mask with some apprehension. Svenna was certainly much larger than Melindwr had been, and quite a different colour. She was a beautiful grey-blue all over, her chest horizontal bars of soft grey and white feathers. She looked at Humphrey out of the packing case with a round speculative golden eye.

"How savage is she?" I wondered. I could see Svenna looking speculatively at me too.

"If one is once going to start wearing armour to deal with a hawk, one might as well not have a hawk," Humphrey decided. So we put the mask carefully away. Even so, Humphrey handled Svenna with gingerly circumspection. She was already jessed and belled, and as she was half trained I felt we should not have to endure the terrible waking programme all over again.

Humphrey thought he might have to wake her for one night, but Svenna proved herself already well manned. She stepped daintily out of her case on to Humphrey's gloved fist, while I stood well back in case one of those steel-tipped feet should flash out in my direction. Svenna didn't even look at me and Humphrey carried her carefully round the garden. For daytime we made her a movable perch out of an old gong-stand, with a long curtain of striped green and white blind awning, which gave a bizarre appearance to our back yard. Humphrey also got the blacksmith to make some garden perches, which he stuck into the grass. These were hoop perches with a heavy padded leather top. It was cold that winter also, and there was usually snow on the ground. Svenna got quite used to sitting out on her perch stuck into the snow-covered flower bed, enjoying the early morning sunshine.

By January we had Svenna hunting. Humphrey took her out an hour after her normal feeding time, her head bobbing up and down on a stalk, watching each dry tuft of grass for a resting hare, and peering at hedges as if she suspected a rabbit or pheasant would come shooting out. Humphrey didn't catch any hares with her that first season, but she became very adept at pursuing and catching rabbits, and even moorhens.

One day in late February, when the evenings were beginning to lengthen again, Humphrey and I were down in the Carse with Svenna. The light was just beginning to fade, but as we came round the corner of the Oldwood ditch a moorhen got up at Humphrey's feet. Svenna, sitting on his fist, her leash and swivel already released so she was ready to fly, was bobbing her head, standing on tiptoe, her great shoulders hunched forward. I could feel Humphrey quivering with excitement, sharing Svenna's lust for the prey, so that their minds and thoughts were harnessed on the same object, the same desire.

"Shoo ha ha," he cried, which is the traditional falconer's cry, and threw Svenna after the moorhen.

She needed no throwing. Her short but powerful wings spread wide, her head outstretched, her murderous claws tingling with the anticipation of the kill, she swept after the moorhen, over the bank and out of our vision.

Humphrey ran after her, and I followed, but by the time we had raced up the drying yellow couch grass of the bank and jumped over the Pow ditch, there was no sign of her. Humphrey ran on towards the road where stood Wheatlands, one of the Kilspindie houses, in which lived old Mrs. Tait.

As we got to the road we were surprised to see Mrs. Tait running out of the house towards us. "Oh, Mr. Evans, Mr. Evans, come quick!" she shouted. "There's an eagle on my aspidistra!"

An eagle on her aspidistra? It could only be Svenna. But how on earth had she got through the dark narrow passage into Mrs. Tait's parlour?

We followed Mrs. Tait breathlessly into the house, as she went ahead holding up her oil lamp along the passage and into the parlour, and there sure enough sitting on a vast aspidistra in a brass pot was Svenna.

"I heard this knocking at my door," Mrs. Tait explained, "and when I went to open it two birds flew in, and one of them was an eagle."

The moorhen had flown down the passage hotly pursued by Svenna, dodged cleverly round the aspidistra, and flown out again. Svenna had collapsed on to the first available perch.

"She's a goshawk, not an eagle," Humphrey explained, "and quite tame really." Svenna for once supported this statement by climbing calmly on to his fist, where she proceeded to rouse, and fluff all her feathers, looking like nothing more frightening than an old broody hen.

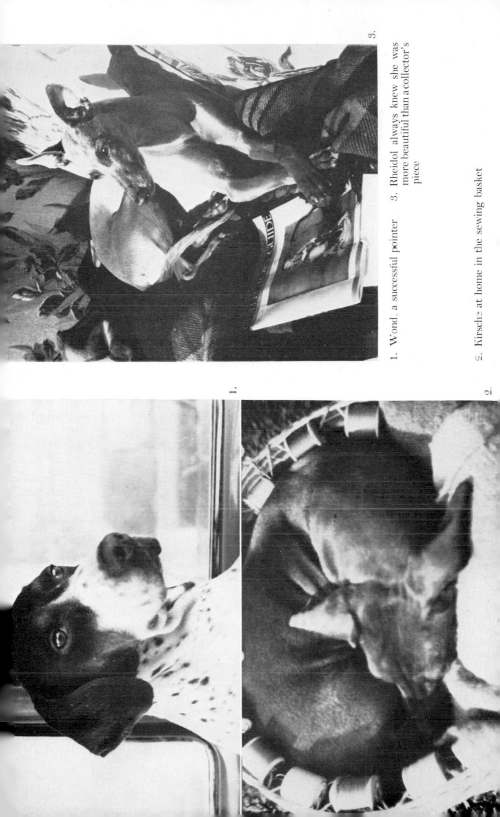

1. Wond a successful pointer

2. Kirsche at home in the sewing basket

3. Rheidol always knew she was more beautiful than a collector's piece

4. Adam on Plum, Humphrey and Charlotte, Garnish, Comfort and Wond in Kilspindie garden

5. Charlotte and Adam help Lady and her 'cairtie' load winter straw into Kilspindie Dovecote

The first time Humphrey went away for a few days leaving me in charge of Svenna, I was terrified. "She must be fed on the fist," Humphrey explained and showed me how to tie and untie the falconer's knot at the end of her leash.

It all sounded very easy until the time actually came. When Humphrey wasn't there it was a very different matter to see a huge and obviously hungry goshawk glowering at me. And Svenna was definitely moody. Several times in the morning when I went outside and opened the doors of the mews, she struck at my bare hand with her foot, which whipped out like lightning when I wasn't looking. She only nicked the edge of my wrist once, and after that I was on the look out for her. At other times she would chirp and twitter like a small sparrow. She was a most unpredictable hawk.

It was early afternoon, and I still had not fed Svenna. I took the carefully cut ration of rabbit out of the fridge and left it to warm up and thaw out thoroughly in the sunshine. Every time I passed the Mews, Svenna changed her feet, so that the bells jangled slightly, hunched her predatory shoulders and gazed at me with unblinking eyes. She was just as conscious of the fact that it was feeding time as I was. Eventually I plucked up courage, put the falconry glove on my left hand, and fetched the bit of rabbit, which I held behind my back so Svenna should not bate off before I was ready for her. Hawks are always carried on the left hand, so as to leave the right hand free for managing the reins of the horse, or whatever else needs coping with.

Svenna was standing fearsomely on her tiptoes, balanced on her branch, and swaying slightly. I went up to her, talking to her softly in an effort to distract her attention from the fact that it was feeding time, and with my right hand untied the leash from the branch. Then, carefully holding the ends of the leash in my right hand, I stepped back and held up my left arm with the rabbit in the glove. Svenna bobbed her head up and down as she always did before taking off, and then roused herself by ruffling up and down all her feathers. A hawk should rouse herself three times before she is ready to be flown at quarry. However Svenna let her feathers gradually subside, and then un-believably launched her two-and-a-half-pound weight at my fist. For a second my view was blocked by a flurry of grey and white feathers, by two hypnotic yellow eyes, then the full weight of her landed on my glove.

As she started to feed, I could feel her talons gripping round the strong fingers of the glove, and I was glad it was so thick. As soon as she had landed on her food, she paid no further attention to me, but mantled—fluffed all her feathers—over it, and ate greedily, pulling off bits of fur and throwing them aside. From under her mound of feathers she gazed suspiciously and jealously at me from time to time, but continued to eat. When she had finished she feaked—wiped her beak—along the edges of the glove, exactly like any old parrot.

When I got to know Svenna better she would let me pick out choice morsels from among her food, and offer it to her ready beak, and would take it as gently as a pigeon feeding from its mother. Except for eagles, most hawks do not strike with their beaks: it is their talons which are dangerous.

Svenna soon became as used to me as she was to Humphrey, and would chirp in the morning like a sparrow when I came into the Mews to take her out and put her on her perch in the garden in the sun, or even sometimes in the afternoons when I took her out for a walk on my fist. I talked to her a lot, for I felt goshawks should have companionship, and Kirsche and Rheidol ran in and out the lanes at my feet. Svenna was in-clined to view Kirsche with an old-fashioned look: I think she suspected she was really some kind of rabbit being kept from her.

We had been in our house now for nearly two years, and the garden still wasn't what we had hoped for it. However this year we became really desperate, and Jimmy Shields came to work for us. He was not a professional gardener, but he was keen and enthusiastic, and between all of us we suddenly began to make an appreciable difference in the appearance of the place. In the first instance we thinned out some of the old apple and pear trees which grew in tangled lines all over the orchard. We left the older and bigger ones, only cutting those which were an unattractive shape. Next Jimmy hand-dug the whole garden, clearing out the last remains of the nettle roots, and we sowed grass seed everywhere to make a vast lawn.

To the west of the house were two large rose beds bordered with a box hedge, tenanted by a dark red damask rose with a delicious scent, and two white roses which had managed to come up through the jungle. A lot of farmyard manure went on, and I bought a collection of roses and planted them. There was already a warm apricot Gloire de Dijon rose outside the nursery window, and I planted a few more climbers round the house, and as many herbaceous plants as I could beg from friends in a long border we dug below the top wall. Jimmy also dug paths and we filled them with grey gravel. Altogether things were beginning to look up.

Our major work this summer was the diversion of the Kilspindie Burn which ran through the garden and the construction of two garden ponds. Humphrey and Jimmy Shields dug out a new course for the stream, meandering it across the top of the orchard and into a small pond, using the earth they dug out of it to make a bank at the lower end. From here the water was piped down to the bottom end of the garden where a huge pool was dug—never deeper than two feet, but circular and about thirty feet in diameter. Both these ponds we lined with concrete, which we painted pale blue. As a matter of fact, this was rather a waste, because in no time it all became black and covered with mud and pond weeds.

In the late summer evenings Humphrey and I went out fishing for trout to stock the pond. They weren't very big trout, and we mostly caught them in the little burns running between the shoulders of the Sidlaw Hills. I say we caught them, but it was Humphrey who did the fishing: I just stood ready with the blue and white nappy pail.

Up there, we could see right across the great plain of the Carse of Gowrie to the blue hills of Fife the other side of the Tay—Norman Law, the two Lomonds of Fife, twin volcanic peaks, and always beneath them the wide grey ribbon of the Tay. Out to the east we could see the sprawling town of Dundee, topped by its ancient hill fort, and snaking southwards across the Tay the narrow black line of the Tay Bridge. As the dusk gathered, trains wriggled their way across like lighted necklaces, and the city lights of Dundee began to sparkle. To the west the whole sky was rosy, and suddenly from the thick beds of rose-bay willow-herb where we stood, we heard the soft plop-plop of trout rising in the mountain reservoir.

Like a cobweb thrown across the pink water, Humphrey's line flicked downwards, the fly hovered for a moment over the pond and then was grabbed by a greedy trout. Carefully, gently, Humphrey played him, reeling in the line, pulling ever nearer to the bank, then slipped his hands into the cool water and pulled out the wriggling silvery body. Cautiously he opened the pink gasping mouth, and eased back the hook.

"He'll do," he said, "Hardly touched, only just hooked him," and one more trout was slipped into the pail and the lid popped on.

It was sometimes a long walk down the slopes of the hills, carrying the heavy slopping water-and-trout-filled pail between us, but I loved it, looking in the dusk at the faintly luminous blue harebells—the bluebells of Scotland, on hair-fine stems—the thick cushiony heads of blue and mauve scabious and the pink and white carpets of milfoil with their feathery leaves. Below us were the lights of civilization and the plain, but up here it was as it had always been—the wild flowers, the sudden scuttling animals and the owls winging their way across the evening for their nightly depredations.

Slipping on the steep soft earth we crept under the gnarled hawthorn trees, perhaps here when Thomas the Rhymer walked these hills and was spirited away for seven years by the Faerie Queen. In the Bay of Invergowrie in the Tay is a large rock called the Knowes of Gowrie. About it True Thomas said:

"When the Knowes of Gowrie come to land
The crack of doom is near at hand."

Dundee Corporation is tipping rubbish into the Tay gradually nearer and nearer to that rock, but fortunately there is still some way to go.

It was usually dark by the time we got back to the garden and going down to the bottom gradually released the pail at the edge of the pond. One by one the trout slid slowly out of their container, and then with a flicker of their tail fins, swam into the deeper water in the middle.

By the end of the summer we had the bottom pond well stocked with trout.

But it was a sad summer for us, because while I was away at the sea with the children, Rheidol died. She was thirteen and an old dog with a bad heart, and there was nothing we could have done. I had only loved her for five years, but Humphrey had brought her up since she was a tiny puppy; she had been very much his dog, and although she tolerated me her whole life was centred on her master. We buried her by the top pool and planted a weeping cherry tree by her grave. I like to think that sometimes in the long summer evenings, the ghost of a small grey whippet comes slipping through the apple trees and plays in the garden where she was once so happy.

.   .   .

One day we had a letter from Humphrey's father. He told us that he had bought a piebald New Forest pony called Kitty. For two years he had watched her trotting round the streets of London drawing a little cart with bay trees and potting out plants on it. Gradually he had made her acquaintance, and one day he had bought her from the owner. He felt she would do splendidly for Adam and Charlotte.

Adam was only three at the time, and Charlotte barely a year, so we felt it might be some time before they were riding. However we were delighted at the idea of Kitty joining us, and arranged a mating for her with a pedigree Shetland stallion near Cupar in Fife. It was a very cold day in April when we planned to fetch Kitty. She had been sent by train from

London to Cupar, and we had heard of her arrival there, but nothing more.

Humphrey borrowed the Estate lorry, I wrapped Adam and Charlotte up well in jerseys and coats, and we set out. It was an old lorry and had great gaps at the sides where the draughts and cold winds whistled through, with occasional flurries of snow, but fortunately there was some heat off the engine, which was in the cab. We drove bucketing along, the noise precluding all forms of conversation, shuddering and banging and changing gear as we crept up hills.

Cupar is in the middle of Fife, that "beggar's coat with golden fringes", and the cottage we were going to was just beyond, between Cupar and Peat Inn. It stood well back from the road, screened by a large unkempt hedge, and in a field behind five or six small Shetland ponies nibbled the remains of the yellowed winter grass. In Scotland there is not often much bite in the grass until May is well with us.

Humphrey reversed the lorry back off the road, and came round to open the door for us. Charlotte was balanced against it, and fell face first into the gritty road. We rushed to pick her up; she was not much hurt, but had grazed her face, and was bleeding, dirty and shocked. The old man who looked after the ponies came out of his house, and pressed us to come in. It was a cold bare house, with no hot water, for the black kitchen range was unlit, and there was little comfort in it. Charlotte sat on my lap, and screamed and screamed, while he filled a tin mug with water from the slow dripping tap, and I bathed her face with my dirty handkerchief. It was bleak in the house, and we were sorry for him, but in the old shed which served as a stable all was warm and well kept.

He showed us his Shetland stallion, the future father of Kitty's foal. "A wee beauty," he kept saying. We agreed with him.

Then Kitty came out, black and white and with a knowing look in her eyes, and we could look at no one else. Even Charlotte cheered up and forgot her scratched face. Humphrey took Kitty by the halter and led her easily up the ramp into the lorry. We put up the back, battened her down, and were ready to leave. The drive back was just as cold, just as bumpy, just as snowy, but this time we could hear Kitty's little hoofs banging about in the back, and we felt quite different.

For a long time afterwards we remembered that cold bleak cottage, and the warm stable with the much loved Shetland pony inside. Someone told us years later that the old man had committed suicide. Now the roof of the house has fallen in, and the hedge has grown up beyond the windows, but there are still ponies in the field, long-coated and black, and much loved by someone.

We took Kitty out at Kilspindie, and put her into the Dove-cote Field. At first she seemed a little surprised at so much freedom, but she soon got to know us, and came running out when we brought her hay. Certainly she seemed a little lonely. So I was not surprised when one day Humphrey looked up from reading the small ads in our local paper, and said, "I have found a friend for Kitty."

"What sort of friend?" I asked cautiously.

He showed me the advertisement. The friend was a donkey called Bessie. We were all enchanted, everyone had always wanted to own a donkey, and Adam lost no time in running out to the field to tell Kitty of the treat in store for her.

Once more we all climbed into the decrepit old lorry, but this time it was May, all the trees in tender leaf, the roadsides lined with golden tasselled laburnums, gardens bright with daffodils and polyanthus, and white snowdrifts of wild gean drifting across the woods. We drove north this time to Montrose on the coast. Here we met Bessie. She was milk-chocolate coloured with melting eyes, a large donkey certainly, but we thought the most beautiful we had ever seen. There was, it is true, a certain difficulty when we loaded her, but this we felt sure was because she had been ill-treated. This time our long-suffering nanny, Christian Hodge, was with us; no mishap befell Charlotte, and we all drove home enchanted with our new acquisition.

The process of disillusionment was slow, but complete.

The first thing that happened was that Bessie gave Humphrey a very nasty and unexpected bite as he was leading her down the ramp into the Dovecote Field. Kitty came racing down, small hoofs thudding, from the gorse and broom bushes at the top, whinnying her excitement and greetings. We left them to make friends, and went indoors to tie up Humphrey's arm.

For some weeks all was peaceful in the Dovecote Field, then one day Humphrey said, "The grass needs a chance to grow; we'll move Kitty and Bessie into the field below the house."

Kitty had always come running when we called her; she had been amenable and easy to catch. Now for the first time she jinked away when we got near her. It was plain that she had been learning bad habits from Bessie. However we caught Kitty in the end, and led her peaceably enough into the lower field. Bessie would not be caught, under any circumstances, and had to be driven, kicking viciously all the way. We had put our clothes line in this field, and Christian was not very pleased the next morning to find Bessie rapidly consuming a whole row of clean washing. Reluctantly we went into the whole cowboy process in reverse, and herded Kitty and Bessie back into the Dovecote Field.

Alas, Bessie had tasted freedom and washing. She was not going to settle for any old five-acre field now. However we mended our fences, tautening up the wires, blocking the corners with bundles of gorse, Kitty and Bessie defeated us and got out. We felt that our days of running over the countryside chasing stray animals were finished with the departure of Brownie and her Friends. Kitty and Bessie were far worse. For one thing they went faster, for another Bessie bit and kicked. Kitty could be ridden back, at least, but nobody could stay on Bessie. Humphrey and I both tried. She had a buck like a circus mule. In the end when we saw Bessie curling her lips back over her long yellow teeth and flashing the whites of her eyes at us, we knew to keep well clear.

September is one of the loveliest months in Scotland. All the gardens are full of summer flowers, the dahlias untouched by frost, and the days are long and golden falling into a blue haze in the earlier evenings. It was in September that Wond came to us. She was liver and white, nicely spotted, a Brodrick pointer called Isle of Arran Wond. She came labelled in a crate to Perth Station, aged sixteen months. Her nose was soft mushroom pink, and her eyes the colour of peat pools. She came earlier than we expected, and we had to take her with us when we went down for a weekend to the Borders. She took to the car very readily, almost as if she had inherited the faculty from Rheidol, and curled up quite at home on the front seat. On the way down I caught forty-two ticks on her, and we left her in a kennel the first night, not knowing how house-trained she was. She was not in fact house-trained at all, but she simply hated that kennel. No one could sleep a wink all night because of Wond's loud and screaming voice. We curtailed our visit, and took Wond home with us. The next night she spent in our bed.

She soon became house-trained, and Kirsche reluctantly accepted her as one of the family. At first she was unsure of her size, unused to all the tiny things which sit about in houses in the way of pointers' tails, but she soon learnt to abandon her youthful exuberance. There were only two things in fact she didn't learn: one was to walk with any confidence on a slippery linoleum floor, the other was how to point.

I found Humphrey composing an advertisement to our local paper.

"Nicely spotted affectionate pointer bitch for sale . . ."

"But we haven't got a nicely spotted affectionate pointer bitch to sell," I protested. "There's only Wond, and she's part of our family."

"We can't afford to keep a pointer who doesn't point," Humphrey argued. "Wond was only got in the first place to be a hawking dog, to go out with Svenna. I need a dog who points at game, and then flushes it for the hawk. If she doesn't point, then she's useless."

We walked round and round the fields with Wond, and she

41

ran about in a wild and untrained way, sniffing and wagging her tail. As far as she was concerned, she might have been a Dalmation.

"How do you teach a dog to point?" I kept asking Humphrey. "Surely there must be something we can do?"

"It comes naturally," Humphrey explained to me, "or not at all. And I'm very much afraid that Wond is no good, and that's why she was sold at sixteen months."

Humphrey and Wond were out on the morning the advertisement appeared in the paper. It looked worse than ever in print, and I had three telephone calls about her that morning. I was evasive to them all, though I noted down names and addresses, because I knew Humphrey would never be able to part with Wond when it came to the point. But I was certainly worried.

However, I needn't have been. Humphrey and Wond returned triumphant at lunch time. "She pointed!" Humphrey exclaimed. "She made a beautiful point in the middle of a field, on three legs with one foot tucked up in front of her. It was a classic point—quite beautiful."

"Three people rang up this morning wanting to buy her," I said quietly.

"Ah well," Humphrey said, picking her up in his arms. "She wouldn't have gone anyway—we all knew that. But it's nice that she can point."

October was wild and windy that year, and one night the storm swept down on us from the north, swaying the boughs of the apple trees in the orchard, scattering the twigs, and howling round the chimneys of the house. Curious, I thought, snuggling into bed, surely that was a duck quacking above the noise of the wind. However, I pulled the bedclothes closer round my ears, and took no notice. I hate the howling wind at night.

In the morning when we went out to see what damage had been done in the night, the entire orchard was littered with fallen broken twigs, leaves were scattered like confetti, and two big branches had come off one of the apple trees by the bottom pool.

As we went out to investigate we heard a frantic quacking from the pool, and up raced a brown Khaki Campbell duck. She appeared to be hungry, was quite tame, and very pleased to see us.

"Let's call her Jemima," Adam suggested. "She's the wrong colour for Jemima Puddleduck but she's the right shape and she makes the right noise."

We rang up all the farmers in the neighbourhood to see if they had lost a Khaki Campbell duck, but no one claimed Jemima. Apparently she had blown in on the storm out of no-where. At any rate, she had blown in to stay. She soon claimed the rough ground by the bottom pool as her territory, and spent her time there very happily digging about for things to eat. Every morning she came running fast accross the lawn, her wings outspread, rather like a penguin, screaming to be fed. She soon learnt about Svenna, and gave her a wide berth, the hens knew that she was non-competitive and non-battly, and the moorhens who lived round the pool accepted her as a new leader figure. Jemima had found a home.

It wasn't for over a year that we learnt that she had blown in the storm right down over the hills from The Shanry, a farm way back over the hill from us. We often pictured her, poor non-flying duck, being swept downwards on the wings of the hurricane. How thankful she must have been to drop her wings and run for shelter under the threshing boughs of our apple orchard!

With Jemima's storm came winter, and Jimmy put up pens and runs for the hens in the field below the house, Svenna's mews became filled with hay for Kitty and Bessie, we stored apples all over the linen cupboard and the children's bathroom, and one evening in December we found a hare run over on the road.

It was late, but Humphrey stopped the car, for with a hawk and two dogs any food is more than welcome. He got out and bent over the hare.

"She's alive," he said. "I don't know what's wrong, but her leg seems to be broken."

43

Very carefully and gently he lifted her into the car, and put her on the floor at my feet. I held her down firmly, so that she could not jump all over the car. She was warm and soft and terrified, and she screamed all the way home. We thought that when the car door was shut, and the light out, she might scream less. But she did not. Fear, and her sore leg and the close proximity and smell of human beings had combined to terrify her unreasonably. Her back leg was mangled and bleeding, but there was nothing we could do then without making her die of fright. Humphrey filled an orange box with hay, put a few carrots inside it, and shut her in, firmly covered up with hay.

"We can only harm her worse while she's so frightened and shocked," he said. "If she survives the night in a warm dark place by herself, she might stand a chance."

We went to bed without much hope, but when Humphrey cautiously opened the hay box in the morning, the hare was still alive. He took her gently from the basket, her great eyes still liquid with fear, but not so terror-stricken as she had been last night, and examined her leg. It had been broken right at the joint, and was squashed into a bloody pulp, only joined to the upper leg by skin and splinters of bone and torn fur.

"Fetch the kitchen scissors," Humphrey said. "And some warm water and Dettol."

I put warm water into a bowl, got cotton wool, scissors and sticky tape. Humphrey snipped off the last remains of the leg, gently bathed the poor stump and tied the whole thing tightly with lint and sticking plaster. I held the poor hare in my arms while he did so. Then we put her back in her hay box with more carrots, some water and sliced turnip. We pushed the box into the darkness of the wash-house and shut the door.

"There's nothing more we can do," Humphrey said, "Just hope that dark and rest and food will cure her."

We kept her shut tight in that box for three days, and after the first day she began to nibble at the food we left in with her. We never tried to tame her, or accustom her to human beings, because we felt the shock of her accident had been sufficient for her to get over without additional fears. At the end of three days she was eating quite well, and obviously going to recover. There was nothing more we could do for her, so we put her box in Kitty's and Bessie's field late in the afternoon as twilight was coming down, opened the lid, and left it sideways so she could get out easily. We went down to the bottom corner of the field to watch.

For a time nothing happened, then we saw the questing nose, and long inquisitive ears of the hare coming out. At first she could not understand about the loss of her leg, fell over once or twice, and made burdensome progess. Suddenly she discovered how to hop on three legs. She gave a slight experimental hop, and then as it worked, another. Her ears up twitched for possible danger, then she hopped about ten yards from the box, sat up listening intently, and then, as we still made no sound, began to eat. In the gathering dusk we could hear her sharp hare's teeth tearing at the grass. She fed for about ten minutes, and then hopped experimentally away into the darkness.

I never saw her again, but Humphrey did, once. He came back from a hawking afternoon two years later with a fat pheasant. "Gossie nearly got a hare too," he said, "But I didn't let her fly at it."

"Why not?" I asked.

"She was a huge hare," Humphrey said. "Sleek and fat, and going well. But you see, I knew her personally. She only had three legs."

Chapter 3

Bessie's final escapade was on Christmas day. We were all sitting in my parents' house in that sea of string and coloured paper which characterizes Christmas afternoon. We were all full of lunch, Adam had lost his present list, and Charlotte a teddy bear beneath the mounds of paper, Kirsche was running over the dining room carpet for scraps of turkey, and Wond was quietly demolishing someone's box of peppermint creams behind the Christmas tree. It was that time of day when you feel like sinking into some form of gentle painless oblivion. The telephone rang.

Someone perhaps ringing up with Christmas greetings or messages, I thought, as I slowly made my way to answer it.

"Mrs Evans? This is Cameron of Myreside. I've seen your pony and donkey out in the fields just beyond our house."

"We'll come," I said, "Thank you for telephoning."

I fetched Humphrey, and we put on gumboots, thick coats and a scarf round my ears. We got into the car and sped across the main road and prepared to give chase along those flat square fields which lie down the centre of the Carse. There are few hedges here, only fences, and no trees; the ground which is wet and boggy and in some parts covered with reeds, is intersected by deep Pows or draining ditches. Kitty, black and white, showed up plainly, and beyond her and ahead of her like an evil shadow went the wicked grey Bessie. Abandoning the car we plunged across the wet icy fields, still covered with two inches of snow, which in places had melted into deep icy slush.

The wind howled due east from the North Sea, driving into our faces a freezing sleet which might have come from the steppes of Russia. The further we went across the tundra-like

46

expanse, the further Kitty and Bessie seemed to be from us. We tripped over trunk-like ends of sugar beet left embedded in the mud, slithered across the slush, and called "Kitty! Bessie! Kitty! Bessie!" our voices blown despairingly backwards in the wind. In the end, when it was quite dark, a dim violet light brightened by the sudden showers of sleet, we managed to corner Kitty in the angle of a fence. When Kitty is completely cornered, and knows herself to be so, she suddenly turns gentle and docile, and simply stands waiting for a halter to be slipped on to her. We did not attempt to catch Bessie, because she will not lead even if caught. As we led Kitty up towards Kilspindie over the dim snow-covered fields, a dark suspicious shadow lurked behind us and followed at a discreet distance. We climbed a steep bank, over the road and up the hill road which turns sharply at Kilspindie Burn, and goes on beside the row of ancient yew trees which edge our garden. Kitty led into her field like a lamb, and while I was putting some hay over the fence, the greedy Bessie, unable to resist the temptation, suddenly trotted in behind her. Leaving them to their hay and the shelter of the Dovecote, which we knew they would disdain, we went back to the fire and the remains of the cold turkey.

But we knew, even then, that Bessie's days with us were numbered. Kitty's foal was due in March, but as February arrived she became very cross and bad-tempered, and several times we caught her kicking at Bessie with rolling eyes.

"I think we'd better separate them for the moment," Humphrey said, "In case Bessie does any injury to the foal when it's born. Anyway we'll bring Kitty into the Mews for the actual birth—Svenna will have to move into the Wash-house meantime."

So in mid-February we moved Kitty out of the Dovecote Field into the field below the house. Bessie was furious, and kicked, and ran at us, and tried to impede the process as much as she could. Not so much because she was sorry to lose Kitty's companionship—she could still lean over the fence and shout across the road to her—but because she saw Kitty going into the field where all that delectable washing flapped and waved in the breeze. Kitty seemed quite happy and settled, in no way regretting Bessie's companionship.

One morning in late February Humphrey suddenly shouted from the bedroom window, "Come quick and look out in the field—there's two ponies!"

I rushed to look, and there coming up from the dingle where she must have foaled was a very proud sylph-like Kitty with a tiny leggy teddy bear, pale gold and white and fuzzy all over. Humphrey threw on some clothes and ran out to bring them into the stable while I went down to prepare a hot bran mash. Adam could hardly stand still to get dressed in his excitement.

"Kitty's had a foal! Kitty's had a foal!" he kept shouting.

We asked him at breakfast what he would like it to be called.

"I should like to call him Crockett, after Davy Crockett," Adam said at once. So Crockett the new foal was called.

When he was a week or two old we moved him and Kitty back into the Dovecote Field. Bessie was very angry about the foal, and would sneak quietly up on him and try to get in a quick kick. She and Kitty did not renew the uneasy friendship which had existed between them before.

We all agreed that the time had come for Bessie to go.

"The irresistible Bessie . . ." we advertised her in the local paper. We had many replies to the advertisement, and rejecting the people who ill-advisedly wanted a quiet children's pet, eventually sold her to a man in Broughty Ferry who wanted to breed from her. She was not quite irresistible enough for us.

About this time of year, Humphrey became immersed in exciting catalogues. I wondered what they were, and asked casually if I might see one. They turned out to be for shrimps—for trout feeding—water lilies—for trout shelter—and other sorts of minor pond life. "You remember all those trout we caught last summer," Humphrey said. "Well, I'm going to

6. Once she had learned how, Wond proved a classic pointer

7. Svenna finishing breakfast

8. The author and much-loved basset

make the bottom pond a paradise for them, so that on late summer evenings we shall hear the exciting plop of trout rising in our garden."

We hadn't seen the trout all winter, but though it had been very cold, the running water of the stream had always kept the pond from completely freezing over. Humphrey began to fill in his order for pond life and trout luxuries.

"I shall have to clean the pond before all these things come," he remarked.

Adam and Charlotte were delighted at the idea, and got into their gumboots at once to help. Unfortunately they would wade about in the deeper parts of the pond so that the water slopped over the top. By teatime they were both drenched and filthy all over. I managed to get them in but Humphrey went on paddling about in the pond in the increasing darkness.

I was going to a meeting that night, and wanted to get him in from the pond and dry so he didn't come and drip wet mud all over the house while I was out. "You can't do any more tonight," I said bossily, and managed to persuade him to come in.

It was a cold wet night, and the meeting went on and on as meetings do, so that I was glad to be back at last in our warm hot kitchen. Humphrey handed me a cup of hot soup, and I put my hands round it to warm them.

"I'll run you a bath in the children's bathroom," he said, "And then you can tell me all about the meeting."

Why not our own bathroom, I wondered suspiciously, and went up at once to find out.

The bottom of the bath had been filled with mud. It was very full of water, and swimming round and round in the white porcelain were six large trout.

"I put the mud in to make them feel at home," Humphrey explained. "No self-respecting trout could camouflage itself against white porcelain."

I saw his point, but just the same, I was glad to have my bath in hot clean mud-free water.

49

The children loved the idea of having trout in a bath, and spent hours watching them swimming lazily round, collecting round the back of the draining pipe and fanning their tails, or slowly putting their gills in and out. Sometimes they came up to the surface for air, or made a wild dash round the bath for fun.

Altogether they were in our bath about a week, and during that time we had two casualties—trout who jumped out in the middle of the night on to the bath mat, and were found asphyxiated in the morning. Adam and Charlotte had them for breakfast fried in butter, and said they were very good, but I felt I knew them too well to eat them. It was a relief when the four survivors were put back into their bucket, and released in the new clean pond, full of fresh water snails, and growing plants for trout.

In March our game hens began to lay, and although some of them were shut into the pens Jimmy had made, many of them ran about loose in the garden, roosted at night in the old laurel tree, flying at high speed towards it from the wall below the farm buildings like roosting pheasants, and nested above the rafters of the loose-box, behind the boiler in the wash-house, and pretty well everywhere they could fly to. Like Jemima, they came running screaming for food as soon as we came out of the front door. One day I noticed Adam walking about with two large chickens sitting on his wrist.

"They sit on my wrist just like hawks," he said.

We felt with the warm weather that the time had come to introduce the new pigeons Mr. Macrae had given to me when my goose died. He had been keeping them for me ever since. They were meal and white Birmingham Rollers, and we decided to give them to Adam for his fourth birthday. We got a little green house made for them, with pointed roof and narrow slit windows, and this we carried into our bedroom the day before Adam's birthday, concealing it on the far side of our bed. Cobb and Mrs. Cobb, as we christened them, cooed and talked to each other incessantly all night, so that we were afraid the whole surprise would be spoilt. However Adam never guessed a thing, and when he came running in to see his presents, was overjoyed to tear off the paper and find underneath the little green house. When he saw Cobb and Mrs. Cobb he wanted to let them out at once, but we persuaded him that they should be kept shut in their house long enough for them to consider it home, so that they would always come back to it.

In fact, we kept them immured in their house in our bedroom for about three weeks, and then with great ceremony carried it downstairs, and fixed it up in the laurel trees in the garden. It was a fine sunny day, the white lilacs in bloom, the orchard trees a froth of creamy pink apple blossom, and beneath them a wide expanse of mown lawn, which two years ago would have appeared to us an impossible miracle. The heavy tassels of the laurel blew their drowsy perfume across the shiny leaves as we carefully wedged the pigeons' house into place. Then Humphrey opened the little door at the foot of the dovecote, and peering a little at first, not quite certain what this new freedom had to offer, out came Mr. and Mrs. Cobb. They preened themselves for a moment in the bright spring sunlight, running their soft pink feathers through their beaks and peering uncertainly at us with beady eyes. Cobb roused himself, shook all his feathers vigorously, and then took off into the distant blue sky. Mrs. Cobb followed him. Up and up they soared, tumbling suddenly as Birmingham Rollers do, then regaining their balance, and winging ever more certainly far over the broad sunlit fields of the Carse to the river beyond.

For us all, it was an agonizing moment. Adam clasped his hands and said desolately, "They've gone, for ever."

All we could do was put food on their ledge outside the little house, and wait hopefully. All day we waited, and then in the evening as the light came clearer and longer, and I was digging out bishopweed from the bed of violets below the drawing room window, they suddenly came winging back. Adam ran to fetch Christian, who brought Charlotte out in her dressing-gown, Humphrey came dashing round from the Mews with Svenna on his fist, and paused at the gate as Mr. and Mrs.

51

Cobb, tumbling a little, not quite certain of their balance, dropped out of the evening sky and landed on the perch of their own green house. They had come home.

As the summer progressed they became settled and tamer, and led a quiet domestic existence, swooping down on to the grass below to pick crumbs out of our cake at teatime, and perch on a hand or knee, or any convenient part of the body, to pick untidily and greedily at bread and butter, scattering crumbs in a careless indiscriminate way all over the grass. Two eggs were laid and hatched out into two beautiful babies—a black and white one, very smart and called Magpie, and a pure white one we christened Blanche. Although at first timid and much smaller, the young pigeons soon developed table manners as greedy and bad as their parents.

Along the road from us in a farm cottage at Flawcraig lived Mr. Dunbar and his six children. Mr. Dunbar also had a very old brown pony called Lady whom he drove round in a little "cairtie" selling sacks of firewood and kindling. Ever since last autumn, in fact, when the attractions of Bessie had palled on us, we had coveted Lady as a friend for Kitty. Humphrey had actually entered into treaty with Mr. Dunbar as a prospective purchaser for Lady in October, and the bargain had been concluded. One late October day Lady and her cairtie trotted into our field, and stayed there. Kitty was delighted with her friend; Lady was thrilled to be able to browse as much as she liked without doing much work for it.

However this happy state of affairs was not to last, for Mr. Dunbar could not get the replacement he wanted for Lady, and we had reluctantly to let him have her back for the rest of the winter. But we weren't at all happy about it, for Lady who was sweet and affectionate and very ugly, was also incredibly old, and not really fit to go trotting up and down the road with Mr. Dunbar and six children and the loads of firewood, even if the children sometimes got off, and they all gave her a help on the hills. However to our great joy in April Mr. Dunbar acquired a new and bigger cairtie, and a big strong white pony with a long shaggy coat, and Lady was able to come back to us again.

We used her for carting lawn mowings, autumn leaves or muck out of the ponds, whichever happened to need doing at the time, and she averaged about a day's work a week, which we felt enough. She was so docile and quiet that we saw a beauty even in her ugliness, and her green and red cart was a gay ornament to our garden. She was very happy in her retirement, cropping the sweet spring grass beside Kitty and the leggy young colt, smelling the sweet scent of the gorse and broom which covered the hill like a golden crown, and gazing across the grey farm buildings to the roads her little hoofs had trotted on for so long.

She soon had another friend, nearly as old as herself, though possibly one who had lived soft all his life. He was a small nearly circular woolly Shetland pony called Plum who passed from family to family, greatly loved and petted, as the children grew too big for him. No money ever changed hands with Plum's change of address. He simply came to stay as an honoured guest until the children outgrew him. He was reticent about his age, but certainly the wrong side of twenty. He was of a charming and indolent disposition, liking affection, but realizing shrewdly that food was what counted in this world, and only food. He soon made it clear that although the field was good enough for Kitty and Lady, if any food was going he would naturally prefer to be in the garden, where his face was a convenient height for removing bread and cakes off the table, and that even lawn mowings, though oily in flavour, were sometimes acceptable. Adam and Charlotte were welcome to sit on his back if they cared to, he did not even object to a saddle and bridle, but he did not intend to walk anywhere unless dragged with considerable force. Adam in the end could get Plum to go round the garden at a walking pace, but sometimes Plum considered even this effort too much for him, and would just lie down and refuse to move. He was an ideal pony for small children.

We seemed at this time to be acquiring animals at an alarming rate. I was appalled when Humphrey said one morning, "How would you like to have a basset hound?"

"But we've already got Wond and Kirsche, we don't need any more dogs," I protested. "We've got four ponies, four pigeons, a goshawk, a duck, and goodness knows how many cocks and hens. Not to mention trout," I added darkly. "We don't need any more animals."

"She's only a very small basset hound," Humphrey said ingenuously, "A tiny sweet affectionate little dog called Comfort, hardly bigger than Kirsche. She's arriving at Perth Station this morning."

Not unnaturally I went to the station with him to meet Comfort. When we arrived, we found Comfort had brought her friend Garnish with her. They were a draft of hounds sent up from the Westerby Kennels by Humphrey's friend Eric Morrison to start a small basset hound pack. I had gusesed when Humphrey told me about Comfort that he was breaking something gently to me.

Comfort was basically an Artésien Normand basset, but had been interbred with harrier to make for additional speed. She was about two years old, tricolour, gold and white with a splodge of black on her saddle, and with ears shorter than a pedigree basset, longer in the leg, and with a squarer more beagle face. She was, I had to admit, very beautiful. Poor Garnish was not. She was basically a Vendéen Griffon rough haired and shorter eared, and with one wall eye, injured in some hunting accident long ago. She also had a very loud distinctive cracked voice.

We took them into the nursery on arrival, which surprised them a great deal, and their feet slithered all over the polished linoleum. I imagine they had never been in a house before. Certainly they made enormous pools at once, until the whole room was awash. Christian was horrified.

"They must live in a kennel," she said.

Humphrey and Jimmy built a hound bench in half of the loose-box in the bottom field, which they covered with straw, and fenced in a large enclosure with chain link netting, for them to run about in. Here they were very happy, and occasionally we released them into the garden when we were all there together and able to exercise some form of control over them.

There was only one slight drawback. Next door to our garden stands Kilspindie Church, where every Sunday at twelve o'clock morning service was held. There is an old bell which is rung to hurry worshippers into their pews, and the sound of this bell ringing had a terrible effect on Comfort and Garnish. They sat in their hound paddock, threw their heads back, and howled. We were very distressed about this, and tried everything we could do to stop them, but to no avail. Mr. Beal, the minister, was very nice about it when we apologized to him.

"It makes more noise to hurry people in," he said.

In the spring Svenna started to moult. Humphrey decided to let her moult out properly, and rigged up a proper Mews for her in the loft at Megginch, near the Estate Office. It was fairly derelict, but by blocking up the windows, covering up the holes in the floor, and making a large perch for her in one corner, well hung with sacking, we felt that we had made it as reasonably draught-free and comfortable as any hawk might expect. Humphrey removed Svenna's swivel and leash, and released her into the loft with only her soft leather jesses round her legs. Here she was free to fly about as she pleased, and Humphrey started an intensive course of feeding her up with rich foods to bring the moult on quicker. She soon took to her new quarters and established a goshawk's eyrie on the rafters, from whence she would come swooping down on whoever came in with her food, and unless a hand was put up fairly smartly, she alighted on the highest perch, which was of course the head. We had to go away for a fortnight, but left strict instructions for fresh food to be given to Svenna every day.

When we came back one of the first things Humphrey did was to go up to the loft to look at Svenna. She was sitting hunched in a corner on her perch, not at all herself. Whether she had not always been given fresh food, or whether some obscure disease peculiar to goshawks had attacked her, we did not know. Humphrey realized at once that she was seriously ill. He carefully picked her up on to his gloved fist, and took her with him into the car. While he drove steering with his right hand, he held Svenna on his left, half wrapped up in his coat to keep warm. Halfway up to Kilspindie he had to stop the car. Svenna had a quick seizure or fit and died suddenly, sitting there on his fist with his coat round her.

We buried her in the orchard underneath the giant apple tree with the little sweet red apples. It was a peculiarly suitable place, for less than a month before Svenna had escaped us with her leash and swivel on, and flown straight into the apple tree where the leash had been fortunately tied up. Humphrey climbed into the apple tree, up and up, until he came to the small snapping branches at the top which bent and swayed beneath his weight. He had managed to disentangle the leash from the branches and twigs it was wrapped round and then taking the recalcitrant Svenna on his fist, climbed slowly down, branch by branch, one hand being incapacitated by the heavy restless weight of the goshawk. It was a tree her perch had sat under; she had peered up, twisting her head round backwards, in that contortionist way goshawks have, into the shifting green and gold of the branches. She knew the pink of the apple blossom, the warm crimson of the sweet small apples, the bare shape of the boughs in winter, and their elegance in white snow lace. She had been aloof and sometimes moody, a great hunter, and attached to us by a certain familiarity. It was not love, but a kind of toleration because she was used to us. We sorrowed at the passing of the strange wild hawk from the fiords of Norway, we mourned her flight into darkness.

Grief is at best a sharp emotion, one to be dispersed quickly before it grows into a huge emotional canker in the soul. Poor Svenna was dead, but we had plenty of live winged creatures to think about. Every morning we heard the unmusical voice of Jemima shouting beneath our window for food, and Cobb and

Mrs. Cobb, shepherding their babies, would come tumbling out of the air to land on our window sill, where they would sit among the pale pink Ophelia roses demanding their breakfast, tapping on the window pane with important pigeon beaks or stalking along the top sill and peering impatiently into our bedroom.

Chapter 4

LATER that summer Humphrey and I went to stay with some friends in Brittany, taking Adam with us. We motored leisurely across France and arrived at their honey-coloured manor house by the sea coast three days before their annual church fête, or Kermesse. Immediately we were plunged into that thrill of preparations which distinguish even the most minor of fêtes. Humphrey found himself commandeered on arrival to assist the two sons-in-law who were already hard at it erecting stalls and a stage for Breton dances, and transporting trestle tables, wheels of fortune and rabbit hutches.

"Why the rabbit hutches?" I asked.

"I don't know," Humphrey said. "It must be for some kind of rabbit race." He rushed past me into the field below the house carrying yet another rabbit hutch.

I went back to the production line of "tablet" and similar confections in the kitchen of the two maiden aunts who lived in a small house next door. Dressed in the inevitable black, black hats firmly anchored on their heads, they were indefatigable, two tiny valiant old ladies, bicycling grimly uphill, a huge sack on the back and the handlebars weighted with parcels.

Adam had become submerged in a gang of six grandchildren who ran everywhere, got under everyone's feet and had a perfectly blissful time.

When I grabbed him to put him to bed the night before the Kermesse he was full of confused stories of how rabbits were put in the middle of a vast ring of hutches, and when one could be enticed into your hutch he was your very own.

"And oh Mummy, I just know I'm going to win a rabbit," he sighed blissfully.

I thought no more of it at the time, and the next day was chaotic. I dressed up as a gypsy, borrowed the cook's gold earrings, and told fortunes in French in a small stuffy tent for three hours. So I had little chance to see what was going on at the Kermesse. Occasionally one of the daughters would slip in to bring me some cider, or an ice cream, or a freshly made crêpe or pancake, and through the flap of my tent I caught glimpses of a gang of children, one of whom I imagined was Adam, running round sucking ices and waving balloons.

About five o'clock I packed in. I had lost count how many fortunes I had told, and was absolutely exhausted. The first people I saw as I came out of my tent were Humphrey and Adam, both looking extremely triumphant, and the latter carrying a large black rabbit in his arms.

"Look at Chocolat," he said, "We had to buy lots and lots of tickets, Daddy and me, it had to be the first rabbit that went in, you see, and in the end we got Chocolat."

"But what are you going to do with him?" I asked in horror.

"It's all right. Madame says I can keep him in the hen run."

Chocolat was consequently dumped in the hen run, which was made carefully rabbit proof to prevent his digging his way out under the wire netting. It was true that neither he nor the hens evinced much pleasure at this sharing of their apartment, but at least Chocolat was securely contained for the moment. Exhausted by the heat, the emotions and the fortune telling, we all drove down to the beach and plunged into the sea.

Adam came early into our room the next morning, accompanied by at least two little French boys. "Tante Yvonne says we can give Chocolat some of the shot lettuces."

We took little interest in Chocolat in those days, for he kept Adam and the small French boys out of mischief in their constant search for food for him, while we went sightseeing, and visited friends, and enjoyed ourselves.

Apart from the enormous quantities of food Chocolat seemed to eat, there was a continual battle between the boys and Minou, the kitchen cat, who was also interested in Chocolat, presumably for very different reasons. Black and cunning, she would lurk under the shade of the camellia trees, waiting for a chance moment when one of the children left the gate open. But the boys were aware of Minou's interest, and the reason for it, and the poor cat never really had a sporting chance to get near the rabbit.

As the time for our departure drew near, Humphrey and I naturally supposed that Adam would kindly donate Chocolat to his French friends in the interests of the Entente Cordial. Their parents had other ideas.

"We've got to take Chocolat with us," Adam said as we were trying to pack and stuff quite bulky things into our suitcases where there had already been no room on arrival. "Guy-Bernard's mother says she doesn't want to take him home with her unless it's to eat him. And of course we don't want him eaten."

Humphrey and I glanced at each other. Something like this had been looming over us ever since Chocolat's arrival.

"I suppose he could live in a hutch at the bottom of the garden with the hens and Jemima," Humphrey said slowly.

"But how do we get him back? There may be all sorts of import and export laws about rabbits and myxomatosis," I protested.

We decided just to take Chocolat and see what happened at the Customs when the time came. A very old zip bag was provided for us from our French friends, who were all genuinely relieved to see the responsibility of Chocolat removed from their hands. A large quantity of old lettuces and carrots were generously stuffed into the car to provide food for Chocolat for the two or three days we would be travelling, and finally after a frantic chase Chocolat himself was caught, to the great relief of the hens, and was put into his zip bag, and taken off.

Farewells were said, we all waved and waved, and promised to write, and eventually we drove off across France, Adam bouncing on the seat beside us, a large black rabbit in a zip bag at the back.

It seemed a shame that when we stopped for a picnic lunch

Chocolat was unable to stop also, and partake of some light refreshment by the side of the road. But this was obviously unthinkable unless some foolproof way of preventing his escape were discovered.

We ended by buying a very small red collar and lead from an old woman in a saddler's shop in Rennes. She was sure we wanted it for a cat, although we carefully explained it was a "lapin", and when we eventually brought Chocolat into the shop to be measured for size, this was nearly enough to cause her to burst with laughing.

"Fancy wanting a collar and lead for a rabbit! I had always heard that the English were mad, now I see that it is indeed true."

Undeterred by her scorn we persisted, and now whenever we stopped Chocolat had a run. There were several unattractive traits we discovered about Chocolat, living in such close quarters with him. One was his fantastic appetite; he consumed all the carrots and lettuces in the short interval between leaving the Manoir and stopping for lunch. Keeping Chocolat in food was going to be a difficult and expensive business. The second unpleasant thing was the alarming amount of messes Chocolat managed to make inside his zip bag. Whenever we stopped the car we were able to empty it, and start again reasonably fresh, but there was an unmistakable odour of Rabbit about the car, and despite the constant supply of newspapers, a certain seepage.

That night we stopped at a hotel in the country, and as always in continental hotels they made no difficulty about giving us a room with three beds so as to accommodate Adam. There was also a spacious built-in cabinet de toilette, and insisting on carrying up our own luggage, we soon got Chocolat safely installed there. For a time Adam toyed with the idea of having Chocolat to sleep in bed with him, but Chocolat bit and scratched so savagely that this idea soon had to be abandoned.

"But you must get food for him, Daddy," Adam said sleepily as we turned out the light.

I have often seen old peasants picking grass, delicate herbs and dandelion leaves beside the road, carrying home huge bundles packed into bulky containers. It is a picturesque sight, and I have always felt how nice for some old goats or rabbits to have such thoughtful loving owners. Now as Humphrey and I slunk down the road picking up handfuls of grass and dandelions here and there, stuffing the terrible old zip bag, slinking along the narrow lanes with hedges perched on high banks in the warm summer dusk, we felt anything but picturesque or loving.

By the next morning the entire contents of the zip bag had been demolished by Chocolat, and it took us half an hour to return the cabinet de toilette to its pristine freshness.

As I passed Humphrey heading downstairs towards the dustbins at the back door with yet another suspicious bundle of newspapers, I could see the same thought had ocurred to us both.

"I don't think," Humphrey said, "we should let Chocolat wreck the rest of our French holiday."

"We must consider Chocolat's best interests," I agreed. "I don't feel he is entirely happy with us."

That day we were driving through part of the old magic forest of Broceliande; there were beech trees and oak trees, sun dappled, and sudden grassy spaces with a canopy of blue sky. There were little streams running through mossy banks close carpeted with primrose leaves, and the warm nutty smell of fallen beech masts.

"Don't you think that it would be more fun for Chocolat if we left him in this fairy forest?" Humphrey asked Adam. "He doesn't really like coming with us, and he doesn't care for his zip bag. Here he could eat and eat all day to his heart's content, and drink fresh stream water, and maybe find other rabbits to be friends with him."

"I suppose this might seem rather like heaven for a rabbit," Adam agreed slowly, "and no one could eat him here."

We had driven far from the road along a dusty forest track. There were thickets of bramble, and fairy toadstools growing, and the whole place felt enchanted. We untied Chocolat's collar and lead, and placed beside him a whole new pile of carrots we had purchased that morning. Then we walked slowly away.

When we looked back Chocolat was sitting up, his ears erect, his eyes shining, and his whiskers quivering. He looked indeed an enchanted rabbit in a fairy forest.

"And we've still got Kirsche and Wond, and Comfort and Garnish, and Kitty and Crockett, and Lady and Plum," Humphrey reminded Adam.

"And Cobb and Mrs. Cobb, and Magpie and Blanche," I added.

"And don't forget the hens and Jemima," Adam said happily.

Chapter 5

WE had hardly returned from France—without Chocolat—when the telephone rang. It was a pen friend of Humphrey's called Walter Joynson, who lives near Kinlochard. He was going to Ireland, and could not take his goshawk with him. Could we take her?

We were at the time hawkless, and I did not know if Humphrey could bear to have another goshawk after Svenna. I was hardly prepared for the readiness with which he accepted Walter's offer, and made arrangements to drive over to Loch Ard to fetch her.

Walter is a picturesque bearded figure, who usually wears a kilt or tartan trousers, and he was at this time living in a wooden hut on the hillside some distance behind the Kinlochard Hotel. This goshawk, who was female like Svenna, had also come from Norway, and he told Humphrey how he had set out for the airport to meet her, his pockets bulging with chicken necks which he obtained from the hotel. He had a long wait at the airport and noticed people giving him curious looks as he sat there in the lounge, hens' beaks and long purple wattles protruding from his pocket. They must have looked at him even more curiously afterwards, because as soon as the goshawk arrived in her crate, he had proceeded to get her out, and then feed her in the hot airport lounge.

"She was rather sick," he told Humphrey, "I suppose the flight must have upset her."

She was very tame, smaller than Svenna, and much browner all over, with immature vertical bars on her plumage. Walter had called her Shilloolabeg, or something very like this, which is apparently Gaelic. It means, according to Humphrey, The

9. Charlotte, Adam, Morgan and Wond in the drawing room

10. The huntsman waits for the whipper-in to get full control of the hounds

11. Humphrey always travelled with Morgan in the van

Brown Whirlwind of the Little People, but it is possible we got the translation a bit wrong.

Humphrey drove back from Kinlochard with me sitting beside him, and Shilloolabeg on my fist. She bated once or twice, which I hate in the close confines of a car, but on the whole was much quieter and tamer than Svenna had been. She seemed to possess none of the natural viciousness of Svenna's character. Her only defect was a slight weakening of her left eye, possibly, Walter thought, because she might at some time have flown into a tree. We put Shilloolabeg back into the Mews where Svenna had been, and all of a sudden it seemed right to have a hawk back on the strength.

Walter said he had been flying Shilloolabeg regularly in spite of the moult, so we carried on doing this. She preferred coming back to the lure rather than the fist, which is unusual in a short-wing, but she didn't really like coming back at all. We had several nasty moments when she went off chasing partridges, or even sat in a tree completely ignoring all our attempts to call her down.

Finally one day in mid-September we were down in the woods round Megginch and Humphrey was carrying Shilloolabeg ready trimmed to fly. It was about an hour after her normal feeding time, she had roused and fluffed at least twice, and was bobbing her head about in an interested way. A rabbit got up at our feet from under a hedge and Humphrey released Shilloolabeg at it before she could bate off. She flew straight at it, but as it turned and bolted back into the hedge again, swerved off, and flew up into the branches of an oak tree above our heads. We tried for about half an hour to get her down, but at length she flew into a higher tree. I left Humphrey trying to catch her and walked home. Hawking is a job for which you need a great deal of patience.

Humphrey stayed out till after dark, following Shilloolabeg from tree to tree through the wood. Luckily she did not fly off, and he was able to mark her final perch where she settled down to roost when dusk came. He came back in the early hours of the morning with a bow net which he laid out just below the tree at first light. Shilloolabeg must have heard him setting it out; at any rate she looked at it with a scornful eye, and as soon as it was light enough to see, flew off to another tree. Humphrey had another long unsuccessful day chasing round after her. She must have caught something, because she did not seem at all interested in anything he might offer her to eat. Fortunately she did not leave the wood, so at least he knew where she was.

This whole unsatisfactory business went on for five days, Shilloolabeg always managing to catch something for herself, and moving off whenever Humphrey approached within reach of her. As he came out from a copse of birch trees he heard her bells tinkling in the near distance. He could not see her, however, and seemed to have lost track of her. For about five minutes he searched, and then suddenly to his horror he found her lying dead on the ground in front of him. She was still warm, and seemed to have no marks which could account for her sudden death. We could only conclude that her bad eye had suddenly become worse and she had flown head first into a tree.

Humphrey returned terribly despondent with his dead hawk. "Whatever shall I say to Walter when he comes back? I should never have taken him at his word and flown her."

It was just one of those unfortunate things which happen to the best falconers, and austringers too, but so much the worse when it was someone else's hawk.

Walter came back the next week, and Humphrey telephoned him at once to break the news to him. However Walter had brought lots of hawks back from Ireland with him, and although naturally sad at the loss of Shilloolabeg, was not unduly depressed.

"I'd meant you to keep her anyway," he said generously. "How about a cast of merlins now that she's gone? I've got more hawks than I need here."

A "cast" is a term meaning two hawks. We were delighted at the idea. Walter gave us two young merlins: the male or "jack" merlin was called Toto, the larger and wilder female Piccaninni. Merlins, although so small, have dark eyes, notched beaks, and long wings: they are properly falcons, rather than hawks. They have always been described as the lady's hawk, and when we got Toto and Piccaninni, I saw at once why. They were perfectly sweet little birds, and in no time Toto was quite tame and would fly on to my fist for his food, or swoop and clutch at the lure in mid air exactly like some giant butterfly Piccaninni was much more difficult. We could get her to come neither to the fist nor the lure. After being accustomed to the huge lethal feet of our goshawks, we disregarded the merlins' talons, and flew them almost always without gloves. This was disastrous for our hands which soon became scratched, calloused and torn.

We had the two merlins for about a fortnight when a letter came from Walter. I knew at once it was bad news when Humphrey brought it out to the garden where I was cutting down old herbaceous plants.

"Walter's had terrible disasters with all his hawks," he said. "He wants one of the merlins back."

It was never easy to contact Walter by telephone; however Humphrey at last got through to him, and of course offered to bring back both merlins the very next day. Walter, who is deeply generous, would not hear of it. Of course we must keep one.

It was a reprieve, but the situation was complicated for us because we couldn't decide which to keep. Toto was so tame, and so pretty and sweet that it seemed for a bit as if it must be him, but then we reflected Piccaninni was really a bigger bird, and although she might not be able to catch very much, she was really more physically operational than Toto. She was also very beautiful.

"But Piccaninni's not tame like Toto," I argued.

"That's our fault," Humphrey told me. I could see the decision had already been made to keep Piccaninni. But obviously we could not go on calling her such a long name. After some discussion we changed her name to Morgan, after Morgan le Fay. It was a short merlinish sort of name, and it seemed to suit her.

Humphrey took Toto back to Walter, and then an intensive course of waking Morgan began. She was so small and slight that it hardly seemed worth actually sitting up with her. So instead we brought her perch upstairs to our bedroom, and here she sat for two terrible nights with the light on. I don't sleep at all well with the light on, but I burrowed under the bed-clothes and hoped for the best. Poor Morgan didn't have any bedclothes to burrow under, and for the first night didn't sleep at all. The next night Morgan ignored the light, and tucked her head firmly under her wing. The cosy headless merlin was so at peace with us that even when we walked all round her and talked in loud voices she kept her head under her wing without looking up.

She also stood on one leg.

"You might say," Humphrey remarked, "That Morgan is becoming tamer."

We moved Morgan down to the kitchen, for with the colder autumn nights it seemed unkind to put her out in the Mews, and there she slept headless all night on her perch, with Kirsche snoring gently in her basket beside her. Morgan was not at all sure that Kirsche wasn't some kind of fox, for she peered at her with the greatest distrust. I had read somewhere that merlins are very timid, and often die of apoplexy caused by undue fear of dogs. Although Morgan disliked Kirsche, she never looked like developing apoplexy over her.

Morgan was exceedingly cosy in the kitchen, and took a keen interest in whatever I was cooking. She was so gentle that she would take little bits of raw meat from between our lips, and you could hardly feel her beak removing it. She even developed a taste for little snippets of raw sausage or bacon, and was always delighted to be given a little egg yolk in a coffee spoon.

Humphrey never used gloves with Morgan, and as she gained

confidence in him she dug her feet in less, and in the end would hardly scratch him at all.

At the beginning of October we went down to London for a few days. Christian said she was prepared to look after dogs, ponies, and even Jemima and the hens, but she could not be held responsible for a merlin. So of course Morgan had to come with us.

A goshawk is an impossible kind of bird to have in a car. She is so large, and bates and flaps all over the place, and however many newspapers you put round her, they never seem to be in the actual spot they are needed. A merlin is so small that the whole thing is very different, and indeed comparatively easy.

We had a small travelling block perch made and covered with scraps of green carpet, which we wedged between suitcases on the back seat of the car, well protected with newspapers, and there Morgan sat peering out of the windows and taking an intelligent interest in her surroundings as we drove down. We had also equipped ourselves with an air gun so as to ensure a suitable supply of freshly killed food for her. One of the important things about keeping a delicate hawk in captivity is the absolute necessity for freshly killed food as nearly as possible approximating to her natural diet, and of course for a merlin this was doubly important. Most falconers take their merlins in the summer, train them for a short season and release them again in the autumn, because merlins are reputed to be too delicate to intermew. However we had only had Morgan for such a short time, and we were determined to keep her going if we could.

We stopped in a field for a picnic lunch just north of Belford. Humphrey took Morgan out of the car and handed her to me, and I held her while he flew her on a creance to a piece of pigeon we had brought with us. Morgan was already flying free, and flying well, but knowing how chancy hawks can be we did not want to run the risk of losing her while we were in the middle of a long car journey.

While we had our own lunch we tied Morgan to a gatepost

with a tiring of pigeon's wing to peck at. She was already well fed and merely pulled at the wing feathers in a desultory way, rather as people toy with nuts at the end of a long meal, cracking an occasional one. An adventurous robin came and twittered excitedly on the gate beside her. As all robins are, he was bold and aggressive, and sat much nearer to Morgan with her sharp little feet than I felt was safe. Morgan gave him one or two old-fashioned looks as she peered up from her pigeon-eating activities, but otherwise ignored him. Perhaps the robin knew she was already well fed.

In Newcastle when we stopped for petrol, the car was almost immediately surrounded by small boys who pressed their noses to the window and peered in at Morgan. Morgan gazed back at them unconcernedly.

" 'Scuse me, miss, are you part of a circus?" they asked me.

"No, indeed," I said. "This is just our tame merlin we are taking south with us."

"Is it a hawk?" the elder boy asked.

"Oh yes," I explained. "At least, a falcon. A merlin is the kind of hawk it is."

After that we were careful not to stop in too crowded a centre of population for our petrol supplies. We attracted far too much attention.

In London we stayed with my aunts in Lambeth. They were quite used to our arriving at odd hours with strange animals, and a hawk as small as a merlin caused them no alarm. We were however exceedingly cautious about their cats, of which they had three—Sugar, Coalie and Silver. Even the nicest cat, and Sugar was very nice, can hardly be trusted to ignore absolutely the presence of a small bird in the house. And a tied-up merlin, however savage, has absolutely no defence against a large predatory cat. We placed Morgan's perch, well covered in newspapers, on top of the wardrobe in our bedroom, which even the most agile cat would have some difficulty jumping on to, and kept the door very firmly shut.

Even my aunts were a little surprised the next morning to

see Humphrey coming from their garden with an airgun and a dead sparrow.

"You have quite good rough shooting in the Kennington Road," he remarked.

We spent about three days with my aunts, and then, with Morgan in splendid fettle, set off for the weekend to stay with the Rowleys in Suffolk. Sugar and Coalie and Silver came to see us off, and watched in an interested way as we carried Morgan down on her perch and installed her safely on the back seat of the car. From their point of view our visit had been a disappointing one.

Sir Charles Rowley did not take kindly to visiting dogs, and we had always taken them on our visits with some circumspection, leaving them in the car except for brief outings. There had been, however, one unfortunate occasion when he had found two uninvited dogs eating their dinners in his kitchen, and he always enjoyed chaffing us about this.

We were not therefore surprised when he came smartly to the door and asked, "Have you got any dogs with you this time?"

"Oh no," we said rather shocked. "No dogs at all. We're quite free from all dogs."

Sir Charles didn't exactly disbelieve us, but he remained suspicious, and was delighted the next day to find his suspicions confirmed when he discovered us feeding Morgan on the terrace.

"I *knew* you'd have some animal!" he said triumphantly.

In fact, he rather liked Morgan, and even agreed to be photographed with her sitting quite near him.

"Next time I shall be sure to ask if you've dogs *or* hawks," he said as a parting shot.

We returned home safely without further incident, and I rather think Morgan enjoyed her journey. Kirsche and Wond were very upset at having been left behind. We immediately started clearing and cleaning the garden, and Lady and her cart were pressed into active service. Lady rather liked working

71

again after the long summer rest, and although she never went very far with her cart or even very fast, enjoyed the feeling of usefulness, plodding slowly up the hill loaded with straw or old mud from the bottom pool. Adam and Charlotte spent their time busily helping Humphrey and Jimmy with the cart, though mostly Charlotte rode on it. It was a warm golden October, with a crisp hint of frost in the morning air; we filled the Mews with hay for the ponies in the winter, lagged the rural gas cylinders, and Jimmy built a hound bench in the hound paddock shed for Comfort and Garnish.

It was while he was working on this one day that the telephone rang. I answered it, and the operator said, "Can you take down a telegram?"

I rushed to get a pencil and a piece of paper, and then said "Yes?" inquiringly. I have always had rather a dread of telegrams and it wasn't anyone's birthday.

"It's from Market Harborough," the operator said. "The message reads: HOUNDS ARRIVING PERTH THURSDAY EVENING."

"Did you say hounds?" I inquired suspiciously. "Hounds with an S?"

"Oh yes," said the operator cheerfully. "Would you like a copy?"

"I think I'd better," I agreed.

I could hardly wait till Humphrey came home.

"What does this mean?" I demanded. "Hounds? Plural with an S! Surely we have enough hounds with Comfort and Garnish?"

"I don't know," Humphrey said vaguely. "It's from Eric Morrison, and I suppose he may have said at one time he was sending me another draft of hounds to thicken up the pack. I've rather forgotten. It's only one couple," he added placatingly. He arranged to buy a sack of oatmeal for porridge, and a sack of dried meat, and we lost out on our rural gas wash boiler. At least Charlotte was out of nappies.

In spite of my serious misgivings I had to go to the station at Perth with Humphrey to see exactly what was arriving. We went to the Parcels Arrival Office, which was large and cold and dirty, and it was far worse than I had feared. There in a corner were four enormous filthy black travel-stained dogs. They were tied together in couples, each straining against the leash, and they looked most unhappy.

"If you don't like them we can always send them back," Humphrey said generously.

He had cunningly waited to say this until I had actually seen the hounds, and after that, however large, filthy and obviously unmanageable they were, he knew I would find it impossible to do any such thing.

"Don't be silly," I said. "We can't send them back now."

Humphrey took one couple, and I took the other, and we dragged the recalcitrant hounds along the platform of Perth Station. Humphrey opened the back door of the Borgward van, and we piled them all in. The floor had been filled with straw to make it as much like a hound van as possible, and they were soon very much at home in it. When we got back to Kilspindie we tried to disentangle the various names and labels which, partly chewed, were still attached round their necks, and to identify as far as possible the different hounds. They all looked exactly alike to me, and I despaired of ever being able to tell one from another. However we discovered that two were dogs, and two bitches, and that there was one predominantly white dog, and one predominantly white bitch. The other dog and bitch were both more tricolour. The dogs were called Rambler and Lamport, the bitches Grayling and Grecian. They were all smooth-haired Artésien Normand hounds with a strong harrier cross which showed in their longer legs and shorter ears. None of them looked in the least like Garnish, who was a rough-coated Vendéen Griffon, and anyway had one wall eye, and they all looked twice the size of Comfort.

Looking back, it seems amazing that dogs with such intensely different personal characters, expressions and even appearances could ever have appeared to us to resemble each other in the slightest bit. It is rather like when you meet a whole

73

group of new people, and they all seem remarkably similar, so that you can hardly tell one from another—"Was that Mrs. So and So, or was she the one in the purple hat? No, you *know* she was the one with glasses . . . I thought they both had glasses . . ." And afterwards when you get to know them better, you find it incomprehensible that you could have ever confused one with another.

So it was with us and the hounds. Humphrey got to know them before I did, but soon we all knew them, and could even distinguish their voices one from another.

In order to ensure that everyone got a fair share of food we prepared six dishes individually for them every evening, and called each hound separately out of the paddock to be fed. We discovered after some trial and error that the hounds had, arising out of their different characters, a very definite social order, and if any hound tried to jump the gun or rush out to be fed out of his order of precedence, a very real fight ensued. They mostly had ragged edges to their ears from old bite-marks and Grecian, who seemed older than the others, had a scar of an old bite-mark across her back.

Later when we were going through some hound books Eric Morrison sent us, we discovered that Grecian was Comfort's mother. Neither of them seemed to remember this relationship particularly, but now we knew of it we could see that Comfort had a strong family resemblance, although a more refined and elegant hound.

The leader of the pack was Rambler. He was the large white dog, long in the body, very handsome and exceedingly autocratic in his behaviour. During the whole time we had the hounds there was never any kind of challenge to his leadership. He was quite savage, and wouldn't have stood for one anyway. When we gave them bones, which we did once or twice a week, Rambler usually collected about three and took them away into the shed, where he stood over them on the hound bench growling horribly. He was also fairly possessive about the hound shed, regarding it as his personal kingdom, and he didn't really like anyone going inside when he was there. Although I am not afraid of any dog, and certainly not of Rambler, I would not go into the hound shed without a whip when there were bones about, because Rambler always snarled at me in a way that meant business. Rambler did like Humphrey, and would allow him into the hound shed always. Humphrey sometimes lay in the straw beside him, but Rambler always got up and stood over him snarling. Whether he did this because he felt Humphrey was making some obscure challenge to his own authority, or because he fancied Humphrey was edible, and if so, his property, or just to show that no other hound was to talk to Humphrey while he was there, we never knew.

The second in command was Grayling, the large white bitch. She had a particularly long tail, and very beautiful dark eyes which looked meltingly at you. She was always fed second, and although she never made any attempt to oust Rambler she never stopped barking until she was fed. If she saw us looking out of a window at her she would also bark, hoping for food. Secretly Humphrey and I called her Trixie, though we know that was not a suitable name for a hound.

Grecian came third; she was particularly houndy, and Comfort always disputed her position with her. Once or twice Comfort even won, and rushed out third for her food. But Grecian was heavier and bigger, and also her mother, and although she didn't growl so much and show so many teeth as Comfort, she was older and knew more about biting. Comfort was much the smallest, and had no business to be fourth, but she was such a determined dog, and always put up such a show of savagery and courage that she deserved her position. She was nervous too, and much the fastest of the hounds. Grecian was a great egg-eater; she was always watching her opportunity to get out and find the game hens' nests and wolf the eggs, or else slip into the kitchen for a quick clean up.

Garnish was fifth; she was about the same age and weight as Grecian and could easily have challenged her for third place, but she had too nice and easy-going a temperament to make

75

the challenge. She was a friendly companionable dog, very houndy and with no vice in her.

Poor Lamport was always last. He was long and brown with black markings and much longer ears; he looked far more pedigree basset than any of the others. He was a fantastically stupid dog, and quite incapable of standing up for himself in any way. He could never get over fences, and never thought of getting under, merely waiting in a hopeless way for someone to carry him. He loved people, and being with them, but always rather hung back if there was food in the offing, not because he wasn't just as hungry and greedy as everyone else, simply because he didn't see how he was ever going to get anything. When we gave them a bone each, unless we stood over Lamport in a corner, he was always the first to lose his. Rambler considered him beneath contempt, and didn't even bother to take a bone from him. It was usually Garnish or Grecian or Comfort or someone else who had been dispossessed. Grayling usually got two bones early on, although Rambler would soon come and take one away from her.

We fed the basset hounds, as we did Kirsche and Wond, with porridge made in the wash boiler, which we mixed with a varied diet of dried meat, fresh herrings and occasionally fresh meat. If we found a hare or rabbit run over on the road that also helped to vary it.

Before we were able to hunt the hounds, they had to be exercised, and worked together as a pack. They also had to pay attention to Humphrey, and understand what he meant when he blew his horn. Every morning as soon as it was light, Humphrey took them all out for a walk. The hounds soon became very fit, and so did he. Some mornings if it was particularly nice I went some of the way with him, but he walked too fast, and anyway far further than I could have managed in any comfort.

They went on the road all the way to harden the hound's pads, and usually followed the same route, although sometimes they started going north, and sometimes going south. They usually started north from the farm road, up the steep brae above the Dovecote Field. Lady and Plum watched them, but thought it too much effort to walk up the field beside them. Kitty and Crockett did though. They would canter smartly up to the top corner of the Dovecote Field, and then follow the line of the fence down to the burn at the bottom, and up again to the gap into the Croft Field where they burst through, shaking and rattling the dried broom pods and trotting along the narrow path under the line of the hill by the broom bushes until they came to the head of the little cascade which flows down from a swamp, in spring golden with kingcups and flag irises, but now merely churned up muddy bog. From there they followed the field up as far as it went beside the road, until they saw the hounds going out of sight round the steep corner of the Lady's Brig. Up the hill the hounds went, round that hairpin bend, and the next, and the third steep one at the farm of Balmyre.

After the steep brae above Balmyre the road flattens a bit towards the farm of Evelick with its ruined castle, and the mill dam on the right. Over one of the farm buildings is the ancient stone coat of arms of one of the Lindsays of Evelick, and towering above the Pole Hill, with the sharply defined fort on its extreme edge, which is always called locally the Roman Camp. This is as far as I ever walked with the bassets. From Evelick I could turn and go back down, gazing at the view across the Tay, and taking my own pace down the hill towards Kilspindie. But Humphrey and the bassets went on. The whole walk would be six or seven miles and took them nearly two hours. By then Humphrey was ready for his breakfast, and the hounds quite glad to get back into their run for a long drink of water and a small ration of biscuit.

After about a fortnight's steady hound exercise Humphrey and the hounds felt they knew each other sufficiently to try a small hunt. We started hunting the flat stubble fields below Wheatlands, and I was amazed to see the control Humphrey had over the hounds, and the way he knew their different voices. Even in the hunting field they had different characteristics, and it took time getting to know them. Comfort was inclined to go off after fresh hares; she was much faster than the others, and it was quite an achievement to run after her and bring her back. Garnish, who had an unmistakable and most unharmonious cracked voice, was inclined to hunt independently, and paid least attention of any of the hounds. Lamport often ran mute, or lay in a ditch with his feet collapsed, covered in mud, insisting on being carried.

Adam was an enthusiastic hunt supporter, Charlotte not so much. Her legs got tired, the mud slopped over her little red gumboots, and like Lamport it was not long before she too insisted on being carried. In the end Christian brought her down to watch the start of the hunt, and then took her back again. At first we tried to see whether Adam couldn't ride with the hounds. Crockett was too young, and not yet broken, Kitty was too wild and with too hard a mouth, and Lady really was happier in her cart. So that left us with Plum. In spite of his immense and fantastic age Plum was quite happy to have a saddle and bridle put on him, but when Adam got on to him he decided that that was as much as any pony could be expected to do. Adam was quite unable to make him move in any direction. In the end I had to drag him along, and although we got him down to the flat land in the Carse there was no cantering or galloping about with Plum. He moved, if at all, very very slowly indeed. And I saw him several times looking enviously and meaningly at Lamport whom I was carrying.

"No, Plum," I said firmly. "There are limits."

We were at the time in the fields south of the Pow, just to the north of Oldwood, Humphrey in front running after the hounds who were in full cry after a hare. Comfort, who was in front, suddenly broke off as a fresh hare got up and swung round to the left after it. The other hounds ignored the fresh scent and went on hunting the old line, and Humphrey shouted back to me as he ran after the pack to go after Comfort and rescue her before she got to the main road. I abandoned Adam and Plum, and raced round to the left after Comfort.

She ran up to an intersection of the Pow, and emerged muddy

and still going flat out in full cry on the far side. I managed to jump the ditch, and scrambling up the opposite bank, squeezed under a barbed wire fence. It was now permanent pasture grass underfoot, and I was able to run faster on it. So was Comfort.

She must have run at least half a mile before I caught up with her and was just able to throw myself on to her as she was scrambling through another fence. I made a lead out of my scarf and mackintosh belt tied together and dragged her back triumphantly across the fields towards the brae below Kilspindie. Humphrey and the rest of the pack had disappeared over the rise leading up to Pitroddie, and would not be back for some time, I judged. Adam and Plum were still standing where I had left them. Dragging the reluctant Plum with one hand, and Comfort, now exhausted, with the other, we made our way home. After this attempt we made less effort to include Plum in our meets. Adam said he really got on better without him.

By the end of November hounds were hunting really well, and we held a grand opening meet at Balruddery, north of Invergowrie, by invitation of David Sharp. Below the house, which is set back on the Sidlaws, about nine miles east of Kilspindie, there is a wide expanse of rolling grassland and roots, running down to a wood just north of the main Perth-Dundee road. It was quite an occasion for the hounds, their first proper meet with followers other than family. We met David Sharp below Balruddery and struck out through the policies towards Ladyfield and the Home Farm. Scent was good, it was a lovely day, and the pack behaved beautifully. We had two splendid hunts during the afternoon, although of course we did not catch anything, and then there was a delicious tea provided by David's mother. Altogether a very satisfactory day's outing, we thought as we drove back in the van, hounds lolling muddily and sleepily against each other in the straw at the back.

Our opening meet had been such a success that the next Saturday we were invited by Matthew and Janet White to bring the hounds to hunt the hill country south of Forteviot.

79

We met at Hennhill, Matthew's farm, and then drove along the road to Dunning and up towards Path of Condie. Here we parked the van, and debussed the hounds, who hunted across the north slopes and summits of some of the Ochils, over Matthew's hill farms. It was misty, but the scent was fairly good, and the hounds went well over the very steep terrain. Janet's father and also Humphrey's father, who was a keen supporter, were both on the strength and going well. We had a good day's hunting, the hounds' voices echoing over the green slopes of the hills, and eventually fading into the mist and darkness. One well-known cracked voice was not with us latterly, and when Humphrey called the hounds in we discovered there were only five. Garnish, the independent hunter, had gone off.

However, during tea at Hennhill, Matthew did some telephoning and soon heard of an unidentified dog, which was lying very muddy and dirty by the fire at Middle Third farm. This, we knew, could only be Garnish. She was giving a very fair imitation of a house dog when we met her, but was delighted to see us and rejoin her friends in the van. We drove home in the dark with six muddy hounds curled up in the straw at the back dreaming of hunting and hot dinners to come.

After our two days' invitation hunting we had gained confidence in the behaviour of the hounds. So when Colonel Mick Lindsay telephoned to ask if we would bring the pack out with the Pony Club at the end of December we decided to risk it.

"We've never hunted a drag before," Humphrey explained. "Only live hares."

"Never mind," Mick said. "Bring them over here next Wednesday and we'll have a practice drag and see how they get on."

On Wednesday we packed the hounds into their van and set off for Hallyburton which is north-east of us, just below the northern slopes of the Sidlaws. It was a muggy day, and the scent was practically nil; however we consoled ourselves with the thought that it was only a practice. We started in the park

12. Hesse, the grey goshawk

13. Venom, the killer goshawk

14. Star, the brave sparrowhawk

in front of the house, trying to make them follow a drag laid with hare juice in a sack, and also a dead hare, but the hounds were not in the least interested. They dawdled about and sniffed, Garnish tried a bit of unofficial rabbiting, and, eventually losing confidence in us, they swung off into the woods and hunted live hares individually. Humphrey called them all off and we managed to pack them back into the van.

"I'm sorry," he said to Colonel Lindsay. "I don't think they will hunt a drag."

But Mick Lindsay was still enthusiastic about the idea. "It'll be so much more fun for the children having real hounds to hunt with. I'll get some special wolf messes from the Zoo to lay the drag with, and I'm sure they'll be all right on the day."

We were not so certain; however we had one or two more quite good hunts at Kilspindie, and by the Saturday after Christmas were once more feeling encouraged. We met outside the house at Hallyburton, and there were over thirty mounted followers out, mostly children, though Colonel Lindsay and Janet White were there to give support. We let the hounds out of the van, and they were delighted to see all the spectators and people milling about. They rushed from one to another being ingratiating, all except Rambler, who felt talking to people was a waste of time and when could he get down to the real day's business of hunting.

At last the hunt set off into the field. A drag had been laid across a series of little jumps, and we had our fingers crossed that this time hounds would follow it. Humphrey lifted the hounds down one after another over the haha, and led them to the start of the drag encouragingly. Alas, they paid no attention to it at all, in spite of the very strong scent, and found at once in the park, swinging right-handedly in quite the wrong direction, and setting off at spanking speed towards Ballunie and Baldowrie, in full cry.

They went too fast for Humphrey to keep up with them. However, he hailed Lucy Drummond-Moray who was galloping past, and she reined in, and let him jump on to the back of her horse. The two riders slowed the horse down a bit, but they were still able to keep up with the hounds. Noses to ground and sterns waving, the bassets careered along, closely followed by all the mounted riders who abandoned the carefully set out course and galloped cross country after the hounds as fast as they could go. They hunted the hare so hard that they eventually cornered her in the angle of a dyke, and would have had their first kill of the season. However, everyone shouted so many instructions, and the hounds themselves were so amazed at actually being within striking distance of a hare, that the hare turned, ran straight back through the pack and disappeared, entirely unhurt, leaving the hounds open-mouthed.

The original drag having now been abandoned, they drew on southwards towards Coupar Angus, but did not find again. However it had been a very exciting hunt while it lasted, and it was only when Humphrey called the hounds in to go home that he noticed the absence of someone with a well-known cracked voice. Garnish was missing again.

Humphrey blew his horn, and shouted and whistled, but there was no sign of her at all, and eventually we had to return with five hounds only. It was quite dark by then, and we were all miserable.

Colonel Lindsay assured us that Garnish would be all right: hounds always were, and not to worry. However we did, and passed a disturbed night, thinking of poor Garnish, cold and lost in the woods.

Colonel Lindsay telephoned us on Sunday morning.

"We've found your hound. She turned up at a farm, and they thought she was a stray dog, and took her in. I'll collect her for you, if you'll come round to Hallyburton to pick her up."

We were tremendously relieved, although we both pretended to ourselves that somehow we hadn't been worried, we had known Garnish would fall on her feet. We drove over to Hallyburton after lunch, and when we arrived found a large clean shaggy Sealyham-type dog asleep by the drawing room fire. She rolled over in a sleepy way, disclosing a fat pink tummy, and wagged her tail vaguely.

Apart from routine politeness she was not particularly pleased to see us.

"Well, Garnish," we said. "We might have known that it would be you."

Garnish winked her wall eye at us, to let us know that she was a hound of character who could look after herself. She sat on the front seat between us all the way home, disdaining the straw in the back.

Chapter 6

WE usually spent Christmas with my parents, and while we were there combined with various friends to produce a Christmas pantomine. Our great stand-by was Basil Dean, the producer, who came to stay every year. He was not only extremely funny himself when persuaded on the boards, but invaluable in producing us, and hiding our more amateurish efforts under a veneer of professionalism. This year we decided to do *Cinderella*.

"And I tell you what," I said in a rash moment. "We'll have a real live pony to draw Cinderella's coach. We'll bring Plum down."

"We'd never get him up the stairs," Humphrey said, "and he's far too heavy to carry. Perhaps we could make some kind of hoist, and raise him up in a sling."

Megginch, like many Scottish houses, has all the main living rooms on the first floor. It is a survival of the old lawless days, not so long ago in Scotland, when the ground floor vaulted rooms of the castle were used for driving cattle into when marauders were about. We were going to do our play in the central hall on the first floor, called the Armoury. A flat open roof leads off this to a turret. Here we planned to stable Plum. If, that is, he could be got upstairs.

As the time approached we began to get more and more worried as to whether Plum would ever make the ascent.

"You can't let me down now," my father complained. "I've already converted an old pram into a coach, and sprayed it all with silver glitter. It'll be most effective."

He was standing at the entrance to the undercroft, with a spray gun in his hand, covered in paint and glitter up to his eyebrows, behind him a row of green hardboard Christmas trees, and a vast plaster-of-paris pumpkin.

We filled the turret with straw, and carted up a large trough for water. There was no trouble catching Plum, he was always hanging round the gate waiting to be fed. We slipped a halter on him and gave him to Jimmy to lead down while we went on ahead in the van to make everything ready for him. It was a very tired Plum who eventually walked up to the front door, dragged by Jimmy who was nearly as exhausted. Three miles was definitely beyond Plum's limit of what any pony should be required to walk. We got him up the front door steps and through the front door, his little hoofs echoing sharply on the stone; round the passage he went and up another step which left him opposite the front staircase.

"Now for the sixteen steps," said Humphrey.

He stood in front of Plum, grasping him firmly by the halter and holding an apple just in front of his nose. Plum's lips curled backwards a bit: he took an interest in apples. Adam and Charlotte went futher and further up the stairs holding out bread and sugar and apples, anything they could think of to tempt Plum up. Jimmy and I stood behind, leaning against Plum, and ready to push him up from below. In fact none of our precautions were necessary. Plum, excited by the smell and thought of all that food, walked upstairs without a backward look.

We led him through the double doors at the top, across the Armoury, and out into his own turret. Plum walked gingerly across the leaded roof, inspected his straw stable, and had a long drink of water out of his trough. Then he went back into his own private turret, and settled himself comfortably on the straw.

We were doing two performances of the pantomime, one that afternoon, and one on New Year's Day. My mother, who had had the house filled with people for the last week, had kept a permanent buffet of food on the dining room table. Occasionally plates were cleared and washed up, and fresh food was brought

85

in, but otherwise breakfast seemed to slide into lunch, and lunch into tea, without any diminution of the numbers fed, or the amount of people standing about in the dining room waiting for the next meal.

As soon as we had installed Plum in his new turret stable, Humphrey went downstairs for another load of straw and made a large straw nest in the drawing room for Plum to stand in between appearances. Basil Dean and my father had decided that we were to have the dress rehearsal directly before the first performance that afternoon, so we were all rushed through lunch as early as possible in order to make up and dress in the drawing room.

We had persuaded Basil to be the Dame, and he was a resplendent stepmother in a long mauve tea gown and ostrich feather boa of my mother's, topped by a violet-sprinkled hat. Adam and Charlotte had several quick changes to make, and Christian had their clothes ironed and laid out in a corner near to Plum's straw nest. Plum himself wore bunches of scarlet ribbons tied over his harness, and with his thick winter coat all brushed and long mane looked like an enormous teddy bear.

We ran across the first snag with Plum during the dress rehearsal, for although he was perfectly happy to be harnessed into the coach, nothing would induce him to budge an inch when he was in it. He considered his straw nest perfectly adequate, and saw no need to move out into the corridor with the slippery floor boards.

"Jimmy will have to drag him across," Humphrey decided. "It's the only possible way of making him mobile."

The coach could in fact only go across the stage one way, because the other side was undecorated, and betrayed its origins of broken down old pram. Once Plum had made his splendid entrance, and stood waiting for admiration in the centre of the stage, a part which came naturally to him, he had to be dragged into the dining room by Jimmy, turned, and hurried back into the drawing room during a convenient moment of darkness.

"What is Jimmy going to wear?" Basil asked suddenly. "He will have to be dressed for the part."

Every available costume had been pressed into use. Nobody had a coachman's cape, or a suit of footman's livery handy. However, after some searching we discovered the uniform of a Rear Admiral of 1810, belonging to my great-great-grandfather, which fitted Jimmy perfectly.

We were still only part-dressed, with some people made up and others not, and the dress rehearsal had come to a sticky impasse with a picnic scene in the forest held by the Baroness and the Ugly Sisters when the first children started arriving for the party.

"They can't come now," Basil said crossly. "We must just go on with this scene until we get it right. Now, *you* throw the bread, and *you* throw the ham, Jamie . . . No, *Sandy* throws the bread. We must start again."

Fortunately for everybody, more and more audience started arriving, and the cast shut themselves in the drawing room to finish off their make up. The Ugly Sisters had erected a large screen "to dress behind", but it also concealed the giant bottle of brandy from the dining room, which they had taken with them for safety.

The dress rehearsal might have been a shambles; the real performance went like a dream, and the children in the audience sat open-mouthed as Plum, decked with red ribbons, walked briskly on to the stage dragging the glittering coach with pink candles lit in sockets all round it. The two hours seemed to have gone in no time, and we were removing make-up and costumes, unharnessing Plum, and putting him back in his stable on the roof while the children were busy in the dining room demolishing tea.

After Adam and Charlotte were in bed, Plum fed, and Humphrey had driven home the last children in the Borgward van through the gathering snow, we bathed and changed for dinner, coming down to relax by the fire with glasses of sherry.

It was New Year's Eve, and it is considered lucky in Scotland that the first foot over the threshold on the New Year should be that of a dark-haired man. Perhaps this is a survival of the days when Scotland was largely peopled by Picts, and red-headed or fair men might be plundering bands of Vikings, beaching their long boats on the river below for a night raid of sudden death and burning. Perhaps people felt by some form of symbolism or imitative magic that if the very first foot over the threshold was that of a dark-haired man, so might that hearth be safe for a whole year from the marauding Northmen.

We listened to the chimes of Big Ben on the radio, and then as the last notes of the Old Year died away, Humphrey, who was the darkest-haired man present, ran to the door so as to come in and first foot us. He opened the door in the Armoury leading to the turret roof, and under a slight powdering of snow, in walked our first foot—male, definitely dark, but with four feet.

Plum trotted across the Armoury, and came expectantly into the library where we all stood with newly opened bottles of champagne to toast the New Year. He looked round curiously, but was quite pleased to be with us, and joined in our circle as we linked hands and sang For Auld Lang Syne. Then he wandered round the room picking apples off the table which was conveniently placed for his nose, and being fed with bread and chocolate. He was manoeuvring himself into position to lie down by the fire like a large dog about one in the morning when my mother suggested he should go back to his turret.

"I think," she said, "he should be got back in time before there's an accident on the carpet."

Plum was not at all keen to go, but in the end we managed to push him out. The turret above the front door was warm and sheltered with straw and hay in it, but although we left the door open encouragingly, Plum preferred the open roof and the stars. Long after we were in bed, Humphrey and I could hear Plum's little feet walking about on the roof below our bedroom window.

The second performance of the pantomime on New Year's Day went as smoothly as the first one had done, and afterwards

Plum was the centre of attention in his nest of straw amongst a crowd of admirers.

After the final performance of the pantomime was over, and all our friends gone away, we were left with the débris and tidying up. There was straw all over the drawing room carpet, hired costumes and wigs lying about loose in odd corners, together with personal oddments which had been left behind by the performers—a jersey, a tie, shoes, socks and an eyeglass. The large bottle of brandy had disappeared, but we discovered it before too long in the bedroom shared by the two Ugly Sisters, where they had taken it for safe keeping. In spite of this the level had dropped considerably. And of course there was Plum.

"Plum must go back to his friends on the hill," Humphrey said.

We had never thought how we would get Plum downstairs, only how we could get him up. How on earth was it to be done? We were all exceedingly nervous about the operation, except for Plum himself. Humphrey held tightly on to his head stall, I went in front with some more apples and everyone else came behind, ready to grab if Plum started to escalate.

Plum walked out of the drawing room, and down the seventeen steps as if he were a pony accustomed all his life to walking up and down stairs. Not a joint creaked, not a hair moved out of place. Once safely back on to the gravel outside Jimmy led him slowly back the three miles to Kilspindie where he joined his friends Kitty, Crockett and Lady in the Croft Field. They were very interested to see him, and came rushing up at once whinnying. Whether Plum ever communicated all he had been doing, or kept his thoughts to himself, we were never able to find out.

Once Megginch was straight and all the mess cleared up, we packed up our own belongings and moved back to Kilspindie. One or other of us had of course been going up or down every day to attend to the various animals, but it was not the same as living there. There was so much to take up that we filled the

89

Borgward van (which we called TOM because of its registration number) three times and drove it slowly up the hill to unload yet another pile of stuff into the house.

The animals were all delighted to have us back, particularly the hounds, who came and barked under our bedroom window. We had made a separate paddock round the Dovecote for Kitty, in preparation for her new foal which was due in early March, and here we moved her. She could still see Crockett, Lady and Plum, and communicate with them over the fence, but we felt she would have more privacy and it would make life easier for the foal when it arrived. We had mated Kitty this time with a chestnut Arab stallion called Rashaan who belonged to Mr. Milne in Forfar. Although Crockett had the same black and white colouring as Kitty, he had a very ugly head. We hoped for better things with the new foal.

Tragedy had struck at our pigeons during the Christmas holidays. Poor Blanche had completely disappeared. Whether something had eaten her, she had been shot, or simply gone off, we never knew. Poor Magpie was desolate, and sat lonely and unhappy by himself outside the little green house in the laurel tree. Mr. and Mrs. Cobb were busy nesting inside, and would not let him in. In fact, they were distinctly unpleasant to him.

During November and December we had been flying Morgan regularly at sparrows and starlings, and she had been catching quite a few, but since Christmas the weather deteriorated, and Morgan decided she was really more of a kitchen hawk, and took up permanent residence beside the stove. She would come and sit on her small travelling perch by the drawing room fire in the evening, or accompany us to our bedroom, but that was as far as she went. Knowing of the extreme delicacy of merlins, we were taking no chances of her catching a chill, for we were determined to get her through the winter and flying again next season.

One morning we heard a terrible commotion going on amongst the hounds, growling and snarling and fur flying in every direction. Humphrey rushed out to see what they were doing, and found that several of the hounds had set upon poor little Comfort, and in the scrimmage, her front paw had been bitten in three places.

Humphrey shouted to the hounds, and pushed them off with his foot, though Rambler was snarling in an unattractive and sinister way. I opened the gate of the hound paddock and Humphrey carried Comfort out. She appeared quite incapable of walking, but we discovered this was largely nerves. She was very upset indeed, even when we took her into the kitchen and bathed the paw with warm water and Dettol. After we had sponged it down, and put on some healing ointment which Comfort promptly licked off, we made a cosy place for her in the corner of the kitchen.

"I think she's trying it on," Humphrey said, "but we'll wait a bit before we put her back with the others."

Comfort lay in her corner wagging her tail feebly, only just able to wolf down a little milk and egg. She was too ill a dog to touch anything, she said, but in fact when she saw food coming a covetous gleam appeared in her eye, and she turned out to be not so bad as she had thought. Later in the day she managed to crawl upstairs and collapse under the square piano in our bedroom. I could not think where she had gone to, and was very alarmed when I suddenly found her lying stretched out, apparently completely collapsed, in our bedroom. For a time I feared she was dead, but I saw a cunning basset eye peering at me, as she very feebly wagged her tail, and I realized that it was partly the effort and novelty of walking up stairs which had caused her collapse.

I called Humphrey up to see her, and he was very amused.

"She wants to become a house dog like Wond and Kirsche," he said. "That's all that's wrong with Comfort."

We carried her downstairs again to the kitchen where she spent the rest of the day, but when we found her half inside the bread bin snatching great bites out of the bread we realized that the time had come for her to rejoin the pack. She was quite fit and well again, and able to hunt by Saturday with no ill effects, although she still obviously felt very sorry for herself.

We had three more successful hunts in January over the Kilspindie ground, sometimes hunting eastwards towards Pitroddie, and sometimes southward over Oldwood and the Myres. Besides Matthew White, David Sharp and Humphrey's father, my mother had also become a hunting enthusiast and was often out with us over the flat ground. Adam was very keen, and kept up well, though some of the hunt supporters were nearer the hounds than others. This applied particularly when it was over plough.

Our snowdrops came out, and our Christmas roses, and I began to feel that spring was on the way. Jemima obviously felt so too, for one morning she savagely destroyed all the Christmas roses, scattering them about on the grass like giant snowflakes.

At the beginning of February we had a spectacular hunt on the flat ground by the Grange, which used to be Errol aerodrome. This involved some planning, because at least five owners had to be tackled in order to cover every possible direction the hounds might go. They were all very obliging, although initially worried about the hounds' reactions towards sheep.

"They're not those sort of hounds," Humphrey explained, and when the farmers saw the hounds in action they could see what he meant.

Mr. Grant of Aithmuir was particularly pleased. "All my turnips have been chippit, chippit, chippit by hares. You can catch as many as you like."

We didn't explain that perhaps our basset hounds mightn't catch any. Nor did they, but they gave several a little gentle exercise, and perhaps stirred them temporarily from Mr. Grant's turnips. We started the hounds at New Farm, just below Errol, and worked down towards the Grange. There were too many hares, which was confusing for the hounds, but Grecian and Lamport ran particularly well, and even Comfort had forgotten her sore foot, and was able to grapple with many small dykes which intersect the flat land of the aerodrome. Garnish's voice, cracked and high, could be heard echoing over the rustling reed beds to the south where a few wintering geese and duck huddled in the day-time.

Dusk fell across the wide plain, and the shapes of the rusting hangars loomed sinisterly across the fields, while the sun dipped below the hill of Errol. Clear and high sounded the calling home notes of the hunting horn, and Grecian and Rambler, Grayling and Comfort and Lamport came lolloping homewards to flop in the straw of the hound van, to be joined a minute or two later by an old dog with a wall eye, a cracked voice and mud up to her elbows. Another day's hunting was over.

When we looked out of our window next Saturday morning the whole world was white, and blackbirds sat swinging in the curiously heavy apple trees.

Adam came running into our room. "Isn't it lovely, Mummy? Can I have some bread for the birds?"

Foolishly I agreed. We had little left, but I knew the baker's van always called on Saturday mornings. This Saturday no car could attempt our road. And when I looked in the flour bin I found it was empty.

Luckily for us, the situation was saved by red-haired Mr. Simpson, the farm grieve.

"The baker's van will no' make the road here the day," he said, standing in the whirling snowflakes with powdery white hair. "But my son-in-law thinks he can get his lorry up the hill."

Dramatically, like a figure from a Norse saga, he trudged off into the swirling whiteness.

"We must see to the ponies," Humphrey said pulling on his boots. Fortunately we had brought Kitty down last night when the first few snowflakes started, and stabled her in the small stable near the back door. The other three were up in the Croft Field on top of the hill with only a tin roof and two walls of the old croft to protect them. We drove them, floundering in the cold wet snow, well above our gumboots, into the deep warmth and security of the old Dovecote, already well tenanted with countless pigeons sitting snug in their stone nests. Humphrey carried hay and water, I a bucket of crushed oats. Three snow ponies we found them, standing huddled outside the croft with thick white coats and manes. They were pleased to see us, and especially to see the oats, and for the sake of this followed us into the Dovecote. I do not think they would have come just for the sake of shelter; they were curiously impervious to being soaked through. Plum looked tiny in that icy waste, Crockett and Lady not much bigger.

Back at the house Kitty was already at the door of her stable, whinnying for attention and food. Jemima had waddled through the garden to the field at the back where she joined the hens. We tried to drive her into the shelter of the other half of the stable where the hounds lived, but she would not go. In the end we shut the half door to keep the snow out from the hens, and she must have flown over it, for we found her inside the next morning.

Christian, wrapped against the cold, trudged valiantly down to Pitroddie Post Office for our letters. There she found a queue of people buying in supplies of food, and was able to get butter and tins for us, but there was no bread there either.

I went into the garden which was beautiful, like an enchanted forest, though the snow was deep above my boots, and found that the pigeons' green house had been blown down into the snow. The pigeons were all right. They had taken refuge in the coal cellar. Humphrey rigged up a curtain of rugs which hung, stiff with snow, over the entrance to the back porch, and effectively kept out the howling whirling wind which drove wet snow into every cranny and crevice. What bliss it was to peel off my wet boots, stiff and soaking mackintosh, and sodden gloves, and gradually thaw my aching hands in warm water. Adam and Charlotte sat warm and cosy by the fire, their noses glued to the window watching the swirling whiteness like Kay and Gerda.

We were halfway through lunch when there came a knock

at the door. We looked at each other in amazement. Who could have braved the storm to come to us? Humphrey opened the back door, and there stood Mr. Simpson with the bread in a sack on his back. His son-in-law's lorry had stuck at Inchcoonans, and he had walked the three miles himself carrying the bread for everyone in the village.

"Come in and have a nip," Humphrey invited.

Mr. Simpson shook his head, his face red with snow and whisky. "I've had twa-three nips already. I'll just get on home," he said.

At four o'clock all animals fed and in, we were sitting by a warm fire thinking about tea, when the telephone rang. It was the Kingdom Farm, one of the two dairies on Megginch Estate. Their electricity was cut off; there were only two boys there to hand-milk seventy cows. What could we do?

Humphrey got on to the Electricity Board. They knew of the break and their engineers would be out to fix it. If they could get out.

By six o'clock there was still no electricity.

"Start milking by hand," Humphrey said. "We will come down and help—if we can get to you."

The snow had fallen steadily all day, but had stopped now. It was a clear night with bright stars. It would take us an hour and a half in those conditions to walk to the Kingdom. By car we should do it in ten minutes. Although the snow ploughs had not been out on our roads, I had seen tractors going up and down. TOM should be able to make it. It took us half an hour to dig TOM out from where he stood deep in snow. During that time the haft of the spade broke, and we had to finish with only the blade.

We were confident, even optimistic, of reaching the Kingdom before long. We started TOM, and with the remains of the spade, a brush and buckets of ashes got him out on to the farm road— then we were off. We got about four hundred yards down the hill before we stuck. It was a terrifying drive. The road was rutted with deep intersecting ditches of frozen snow about a

95

foot deep. Piles and drifts of snow lay about like an arctic waste. But TOM was not built for traversing packed snow. One of the smaller crevasses stuck us. We got out and tried to dig TOM out, but it was no use. The small wheels still spun aimlessly round in a deep slough of ice. In the end we had to give up.

"We'll go down to the Post-office and telephone," Humphrey said, "In case the electricity is on again. If it isn't I'll just go on on foot, and you'd better go back. We can try and shift TOM later."

The lights were on in the telephone kiosk, which I felt was a good sign, and we could see lights twinkling across the snowy waste of the Carse.

"Well, that's one good thing," Humphrey said as he came out. "They started milking about ten minutes ago. They'll have finished long before I can get down there. I'll go back and fetch the baby caterpillar tractor, if you dig enough space at the shop for us to turn TOM."

The snow was piled in thick drifts at the shop, but I dug away with the spade and did not feel the cold. The flat expanse of the Carse of Gowrie lay below me in a shimmering veil of whiteness, sparkling in the starlight and lit by the pale light of the waning moon. When I had made enough space to turn at the shop I dug two clear lanes back to the car. There was still no sign of Humphrey and I was beginning to feel cold. It seemed a long time. I started to walk up. Just before I reached the Manse I heard the cheerful put-put of a tractor; Humphrey was coming down the hill towards me.

"I hadn't drained the tractor," he said, "so the water had frozen. You sit in TOM, and guide the wheel and I'll tow you."

I hate being towed, and TOM's wheels seemed to slip all over the place. However, I held tight and hoped for the best. Going downhill towards the shop along the lanes I had dug was comparatively easy, but turning was rather more difficult. However, we managed it in the end, and started on the homeward journey. Charlie, who runs the market garden by the shop, came out of his bungalow to see if we needed help, and up the hill

5. Adam holds Stella, sparrowhawk, and Humphrey Itza, *micrastur semi-torquatus*; Wond doesn't care for either

16. Comfort does not like being bathed in the sink

Mr. and Mrs. Pope and the minister all came out of their houses with offers of help, and to wish us luck.

Up the last steep slippery bit we went, sliding and slithering across the shining snow. My knees felt quite weak when I came out.

"Come and have a bath, and I'll bring you a hot drink in bed," Humphrey said. A small headless merlin was sitting fluffed on one leg on her perch in the kitchen, and the cuckoo clock said half-past ten. We had been out in the cold for over four hours.

Three days later the snows had all melted and disappeared under a watery spring sun, and the floods had come instead at the dairies. One of the byres at Wardheads was flooded, with cows standing hock deep in water. Humphrey dashed down to carry out a major scheme of evacuation—all the cows who were not actually milking being taken over to Oldwood, which was still free from flood water, and the others put into a wet and boggy field until we could get the byre emptied. The level of the stream had risen far above the level of the drains, and the exit pipes were all choked. Fortunately they managed to dig them clear, get the byre drained and the cows back.

We were able to have a good hunt that Saturday on Wardheads and Shipbriggs, with all the hounds going well, and glad to be out after the snow and ice.

Apart from the hounds' habit of howling at the sound of the church bells, they had another curious one we could not break them of: singing at nights. This was particularly eerie. They usually did it when there was a full moon, and the first time we heard them Humphrey and I rushed to our bedroom window to look out. There, sitting in a circle, and baying to the moon, led by Rambler, sat all the hounds, looking as some ancient wolf pack may have done under the cold shadow of the Sidlaw Hills. Their throats stretched into the air, their eyes staring into some far distance, sitting up on their haunches, they hurled their ancient defiance at the pale orb of the moon. Humphrey called their names from the open window, but they ignored him, and went on howling in answer to some primeval challenge from the sky. Carved in stone they were, ancient dogs like the lions on Delos, or the silent stone Anubis guarding the tomb.

We closed the window quietly and left them to their vigil.

A few days after the Wardheads hunt, we noticed that Grecian was not coming as quickly as she should for food. Both Comfort and Garnish had pushed past and had their turns before her, and although of course she could not allow Lamport to go before her, her heart was obviously not in the struggle.

"Grecian looks a bit off colour," Humphrey remarked.

She looked no better the next morning, and we took her into the kitchen and made up a basket in a corner for her. Her coat was staring, and her eyes looked dull and sad. She made no attempt to jump on the table, or dig eggs out of the cupboard. When Mr. Macrae the vet came out he said she had a rupture and would have to be operated on.

With some misgiving, for Grecian was the oldest of the hounds, and the smell of the vet's is always anathema to animals, and often makes them, in a wave of wild unreasoning fear give up all hope of existing, we took her in and left her with him. She was in a large warm cage by herself, with a comfortable bed, plenty of water, and upstairs the soft noise of pigeons cooing and rustling in their loft. It was a place of comfort and luxury for any dog. But she looked at us with such sad reproachful eyes that I could not bear it.

"Come back tomorrow night at the same time, and you will find a very different hound," Mr. Macrae said cheerfully.

We came back the next evening after a sleepless night, and there lying in the kennel as if she were dead was poor Grecian.

"Don't worry, she's not out of the anaesthetic yet," Mr. Macrae consoled us. "It was about time too we did operate on her; we discovered two very bad ruptures. It's a wonder she survived at all with them."

"But she looks as if she's already dead," I said desperately. Grecian's face had that far-away sunk-in look of imminent death about it.

98

"No, no," Mr. Macrae promised. "She'll be all right now. It's still the anaesthetic. Come back again tomorrow."

We went home feeling more miserable than ever, and our hearts were not in it when we fed the other bassets. Rambler came out, and then Grayling, and then with a terrible lurch we saw little Comfort come out.

"Your poor old mum's not at all well," we told her.

Comfort displayed little interest in this, she was only anxious to get to grips with her food. After some late night snarling, all the hounds retired to bed inside their lodge, apparently quite unconscious of the fate of their poor old companion and friend.

But we tossed and turned, unable to hide from ourselves the vision of that poor hound, lying panting and flat out in the hot Dettol-scented surgery. About five o'clock we could bear it no longer, and Humphrey went down to make some tea for us. Soon it was light, and the other hounds were all busy about their daily pursuits, stretching themselves, walking round the hound paddock with tails alert and waving, waiting for their morning walk. But what of poor Grecian? we wondered.

Humphrey had just got back from his hound exercise when the telephone rang. It was Mr. Macrae.

"You can come and pick your doggie up any time," he said. "She's doing fine."

We rushed in to fetch her and brought back a very different dog. At first we tied her into a basket in the kitchen. There she sat whining, wagging her tail, and when she could reach, climbing unasked on to everyone's lap. During her first hour of convalescence she ate a milk pudding, a warm milk drink, three bits of bread and butter, an egg sandwich, two chocolate biscuits and half a cake. After that she felt better still.

It was not long before she was back among the hounds again, a younger fresher dog with a new lease of life, growling and snarling at everyone.

We had not moved Kitty back into her enclosure round the Dovecote since the snow, and one morning in late February when Humphrey went out to exercise the hounds, he saw that there were now two ponies in the stable. The new foal was a very pretty little chestnut filly, finer boned than Crockett, and without that ugly face. Adam and Charlotte were thrilled with her, and called her Goldilocks at once. Somehow the sight of her, all warm and fluffy, fresh and new-born, made us realize that spring was once more with us. She stood close to her mother on long unsteady legs, looking at the world with long-lashed innocent eyes. Kitty turned and nuzzled her with her hairy nose, and then glanced at us and snickered in sudden sympathy as we laid the bowl of hot mash in front of her.

"Clever Kitty, clever old girl," Humphrey said softly, patting her neck, and we looked at the foal again, so new, so suddenly alive, and shared with her mother the miracle of the spring morning.

Chapter 7

BESIDES our six hounds and Wond and Kirsche, Humphrey also shared with my mother the ownership of some greyhounds. As we had no room to keep them, they lived at Megginch with Tom Logie, the gamekeeper. Park Platinum, the fawn brood bitch, had last year had a litter of eleven puppies. Five of these still remained, but were to be sold at Aldridge's in London at the end of March. Being nearly a year old, they were saplings, as they are called in the greyhound world—four dogs, Jet, Comet, Dash and Ritty, and one bitch, Silky. The trainer had talked blithely of sums ranging from £100 to £150 each, which certainly seemed very attractive, and suggested that all five should be sold at once, and we should try to buy in one. Humphrey and my mother decided to buy in Dash, who was the biggest dog, and let the others go.

"Of course a hundred and fifty pounds is ridiculous," my mother said. "But if we get eighty or ninety pounds each we should be doing well."

We planned to send the greyhounds in the train, driving down ourselves the day before in order to be in London to meet them. It all sounded splendid, but unfortunately the whole trip was a disaster from start to finish. It was one of those occasions when every single thing that can go wrong does go wrong.

First of all, Humphrey developed 'flu two days before we were due to start. He must have felt very ill, because I managed to persuade him to stay in bed for a whole day. He lay there, looking wretched, refusing all the little things I put on trays to tempt his appetite. However he had Wond beside him, and when I came up at eleven o'clock with some coffee, I found the sun streaming into the room and Morgan, our merlin, lying sprawled on the bed beside Wond, legless and fluffed out as if she were on her nest. She lay only a few inches from the pointer, her feathers ruffled, every now and then tucking her head down to preen or pull a few feathers from her breast or under her wing through her notched curved beak. She was exactly like an old hen in a dust bath.

"I thought merlins were delicate and didn't survive the winter," I said. Morgan looked sharply round at me, and opened her eye, which was dropping off to sleep.

"Some merlins," said Humphrey.

"We'll have to take Morgan with us when we go south," I said, "and of course Wond, and Adam."

"I don't at the moment," Humphrey remarked, "feel like driving five hundred miles in one go in mid-winter."

"Oh, it'll be lovely," I promised. "We'll take a Thermos of hot coffee, and a Thermos of hot sausages, and we'll buy fresh newly made baps in Jedburgh, and picnic on the Roman Wall."

The sun streamed through the window, the merlin lay with her eyes closed, and the whole prospect began to seem rather exciting.

There was no sun on the morning we started. It was a cold raw day, and raining. Morgan sat crossly on her perch in the back, Wond and Adam squashed in the front seat beside me. We got up at three in the morning, meaning to make an early start, but somehow there proved to be too many things left undone since the night before, and we did not get off till five. We were in Edinburgh by seven, and Jedburgh by half-past eight. There were no baker's shops open.

"Bound to be somewhere to buy fresh baps," Humphrey said, as we drove on south. Beyond Jedburgh is a large tract of wild inhospitable country, most unlikely to have hot baps in bakers' shops. We drove along the Jed Water, up the steep road to Carter Bar where Scotland and England meet, and far to the east beyond the driving rain the fields of Flodden. Suddenly I noticed a small grey van drawn up outside a wayside cottage.

"Stop!" I cried. "A baker's van."

We had already gone several hundred yards past the van, but Humphrey braked at once, turned the car and we drove slowly back. It turned out to be a fish van, filled with raw fish.

"There *is* a Co-operative stores in Otterburn," the driver told us, "They *may* sell bread."

We discussed it half-heartedly as we turned the car and drove on south again. It sounded unlikely, and anyway they would not have the fresh hot baps we had set our hearts on. It hardly seemed worth making the detour off the A 68 on the offchance, so after some discussion we decided against it, and drove across the bleak Northumbrian moors, driven by a biting wind. As we reached the cross roads which intersect the Roman Wall, the wind came howling at us.

"Don't let's stop here," I said. "Let's go on until we can find some bread."

"Not a good day for a picnic," Humphrey agreed.

We stopped at Corbridge, a small grey-walled town with an ancient peel tower in the churchyard. We went inside the church, and sat quiet for a moment, sheltered by the thick stone arches and small deep set windows from the wind outside which streamed across the moors.

"Poor Roman soldiers at Corstopitum," I said. "It must have seemed a long way from the blue Mediterranean and the melon fields of home."

We found some buns in Corbridge; they were warm from the oven and good. We ate them a few miles further south, sitting in the car. Something had gone wrong with the Thermos of coffee, and it was cold and bitter. I had left the sausages cooking in the oven all night so that they were blackened, hard and oozing with fat. We couldn't eat them, but Wond quite liked them.

"At least the buns were good," Humphrey remarked. We were all rather hungry.

We got to Fountains Abbey by lunch time. There were miles

of ornamental gardens and lakes. We walked from the car park to the Abbey, but did not stay long as we noticed Adam was looking peaky and tired, and wondering how much further there would be to walk.

"Lunch should be all right," I said optimistically. "It's hot kedgeree—although I know there's not quite so much fish in it as there should have been. Wond ate most of it as it was cooling on the kitchen table yesterday."

The kedgeree was hot, but tasted oily and stodgy.

"Not one of your days," Humphrey said sadly.

I tried to take a short cut, my map-reading went wrong, and we got lost in Barnsley and Mexborough. Even the Thermos of hot tea was cold. Eventually we arrived at my aunts' house at half past eight, tired out, and very glad to get there. Morgan found her old perch on top of the wardrobe, and Wond came upstairs, one foot after another, casting nervous glances at my aunts' cats, to collapse nervelessly in a heap of rugs at Adam's feet.

By the next afternoon we were fed and warmed and washed, Adam had ridden on the escalators and fed the pigeons in Trafalgar Square, and we all felt quite different. Humphrey and I started out for Euston in good heart to meet the greyhounds. It was still bitterly cold, and as we arrived at the station we heard a long-drawn-out howling in the distance, above the roar of the traffic.

"They must have arrived," I said, and we set out to track them down.

Our poor dogs, filthy and covered in oil and soot after their journey, were being led into a black horrible hole—the only word to describe it—with barred doors. We were horrified, and I got them out and talked to them, while Humphrey dashed about, getting a taxi to take them to the Sale Rooms, dealing with porters and officials. They were pathetically pleased to see us, and jumped all over me, whining and licking me, and looking at me with sad eyes. They all seemed much shaken by their journey.

In a few moments Humphrey was back with an accommodating taxi driver, and packed in first me, then the five dogs, and lastly himself. I had never been in a taxi with five greyhounds before, but they were sweet and sat all over me in the nicest way, so that in the end I hardly knew which was me and which was greyhound.

When we rang the bell at Aldridge's there were two men waiting who came out and opened doors and helped disentangle greyhounds. We got them all out safely, paid off the taxi and led them upstairs to a boiling hot room where men sat round with mugs of steaming tea. Here we removed the dogs' collars and leads, one by one, putting on new leather collars with the catalogue number on it, so that if our dogs did get loose they would not be mixed up. Then we led them into the kennels next door, also steam-heated, warm and commodious, with fresh straw and sawdust in each kennel, and saw them each given bowls of water and a good meal of warm soggy biscuit. They all ate well, except Silky, who seemed to have been most upset by the journey. We left for the night, feeling that they were well cared for and in good hands.

We were soon to be depressed again. The sale was held in a large downstairs sale room, icy cold; bidding was poor and many dogs went for as little as £8 or £9. Humphrey managed to get £30 each for Ritty and Jet, but withdrew the others as the bidding was too low. He then walked them back in the cold to Euston Station, where he had to go through all the business of packing them up for the train home.

Our drive home was even more disastrous than the one down had been, although at least I had organized our food supplies better. We left at half past nine in the morning, and drove through the icy cold to Peterborough, where we had lunch and looked at the Cathedral. Adam looked peaky and tired, slept a great deal, drank some milk, but refused to eat anything. We went to see a man at Tongue End who had steam ploughs, vast primeval giants, standing gaunt and purposeful in the middle of the black fen country. With a hot high tea in Lincoln things began to look up. I had found another interesting Roman road on a map, which we followed but when it petered out in fields, and led us to a deep ford, we realized we could follow it no longer. It took us some time to get back to a tarmac road with signposts. However we got to York, and feeling suddenly cheered, went to the cinema.

It was an unwise thing to do as we were so late anyway. Afterwards we had fish and chips, but forgot to fill up with petrol. By Thirsk we realized our tank was dangerously low, below the empty mark in fact, and no pump in miles. Fortunately we found a police car in Easingwold who told us how to get to a garage. Gratefully we followed the directions, but when we got there found no one about.

"We'll have to stay here for the rest of the night," Humphrey said resignedly. With the engine off the car was beginning to get cold. I didn't relish the prospect. However, we could only have been there ten minutes, when the proprietor drove up in his car, and we were able to fill up with petrol.

From now on we had no more immediate worries, and drove on, in turns, through the night, to arrive home exhausted at seven in the morning, after a twenty-two-hour journey. We carried Adam into the house still asleep, undressed him and popped him into bed, without his eyes opening.

Adam was sick the next day, and had a heavy cold, but he was very glad to be back. The three greyhounds were also sick, but they were glad to be back too.

At last the cold weather began to go. There was no more hunting, for the fields round us were filled with lambs, and the hounds came to appreciate even more their early morning walk over the hill.

We moved Kitty and Goldilocks back into the Dovecote Field with Crockett, Lady and Plum who were all quite pleased to see them, and began to plan a full-scale cowboy party for Adam's fifth birthday.

"I think we should use Lady and her cairtie as a covered wagon," Humphrey decided.

"Oh yes," I said. "And have all the children come as cowboys and cowgirls, and a proper gun fight somewhere, and perhaps Indians, and a cake like a log cabin with those chocolate flakes all over it."

Adam was immensely enthusiastic over the idea, and while I planned the cake and the tea, Humphrey got some iron hoops made at the blacksmiths which would fit over the flat wooden cart. We then decided to pin sheets all over this, which would make an ideal covered wagon. I was quite happy to lend sheets, but drew the line at having Pony Express written on them with black paint, or even flaming arrows fired at them.

One sunny afternoon in the middle of April we caught Lady, and harnessing her into her cart, led her slowly down the road towards Megginch where we planned to hold the party. The sky was blue with rolling white cumulus drifting over the hills of Fife, and plovers wheeling and crying over the new-ploughed fields. Mrs. Pope's garden on the corner of the hill was ablaze with forsythia and daffodils, and Charlie's market garden was a sheet of gold. We had all meant to ride on the cart with Lady, but her feet were long and seemed to be giving her trouble, and she was very thin, so in the end only Adam did.

"I wonder how old Lady is," I remarked to Humphrey. We looked at her teeth, but they were so worn that they gave us no clue at all.

"No wonder she eats her hay so slowly," Humphrey said thoughtfully. "I should say she might be any age between thirty and forty. And she's probably had a hard life."

"Not now," I said. "Not with us."

We gave her carrots to encourage her, but it was more difficult and slower than the journey with Plum had been, and Plum was known to be a good age, and moreover very lazy. Never had the three miles seemed longer or slower. We took Lady along the main road, past all the nodding catkins brushed with golden dust, and the larch trees shimmering in a haze of green, up the drive at Megginch and into the orchard where we unhitched her cart and led her out to the fresh spring grass under the trembling plum blossom. The geese were puddling in a muddy pool at one end, and a blackbird was singing at the top of his voice in a high pear tree. Humphrey fetched some oats for Lady, and we rubbed her down with a wisp of straw, but she still looked very tired and lack-lustre. She drank some water, but made heavy weather of the oats.

When we left her she was lying among the daffodils with the geese chattering round her.

"I'm afraid the party is going to be too much for her," Humphrey said. "We've got two or three days' grace to see if she recovers her strength, but I very much fear we'll have to get Kitty down instead."

"But Kitty can't be separated from Goldilocks," I argued. "She's still feeding her."

"Well, we'll have to have Goldilocks too."

Lady had perked up a little by the next day, but she was still having difficulty with her food, and it was obvious she would not be strong enough to carry twenty or thirty children about in her cart. Goldilocks was too young to lead, and we were seriously worried as to how we were to get her down over the main road, which is always packed with traffic, and only a very small percentage of car drivers understand or care about the difficulties of getting animals across a main road. However we put a halter on Kitty, and led them both down across the fields by Oldwood and the Myres until we came to a gateway leading on to the main road, almost opposite the drive gates. Here Humphrey held Kitty, while Jimmy and I went out into the road and held the traffic up on both sides until we had managed to lead Kitty across, accompanied by a wild and skittish Goldilocks. She was not sure at all about the cars, and kept glancing nervously at them, so that we were extremely relieved to have her safe the other side. We put them both in the orchard with Lady, who was quite pleased to see them again, and snickered a friendly greeting to Kitty.

We left the tying of sheets on to the covered wagon until the birthday itself, for fear of rain, but we were lucky. It was a bright sunny April day, with all the bees out and crocuses and daffodils wide open to the sun. Humphrey, who was to lead the cart, dressed up as a cowboy in jeans and check shirt, and we had Jimmy Shields and Gordon Logie also suitably dressed lying in wait in an ambush ready to be mown down by the horde of cowboys jumping from the cowboy wagon. My father, entering into the spirit of the thing, dressed up as an Indian in the purple feather boa worn by Basil Dean in the Pantomime, and started a large bonfire on the lawn, with several of his guests heavily disguised with lipstick and boot polish dancing round it.

Kitty for once was readily caught, but Goldilocks would not be separated from her, so we had one smart black and white pony drawing the covered wagon, with a fluffy golden foal just two months old prancing along beside her. She was not a bit alarmed by all the children, who thought her adorable, and kept trying to hug and cuddle her. Some liberties she would allow, but Kitty did not really care for them, and curled her lips disagreeably.

The children loved the covered wagon, and we packed about twenty of them inside it, all thoroughly armed with cap pistols, while the rest ran alongside with Goldilocks, and they set off at a spanking pace to the strawberry field where the first ambush was lying in wait for them. Gordon got away, and ran off, still firing—though obviously wounded—into the larch plantation, but after a few fierce initial bursts Jimmy collapsed and lay still among the strawberry runners. Two very brave five-year-olds crept up and took his cap pistol off him, but he never moved, and lay quite still until the Pony Express had disappeared out of sight by the West Lodge.

The Indian party had got a good bonfire going, and were dancing round it singing and shouting. Kitty and Goldilocks were distinctly nervous of the whole affair, and gave it a wide berth, but there was some sporadic shooting from the cowboys until at length the Indians were driven indoors to remove their warpaint for tea.

109

While the children were having tea, Humphrey put Kitty and Goldilocks into the orchard for the night, until we should be able to take them back to Kilspindie the next day. He did not tell me until later, but when he went into the orchard he found Lady dead among the plum blossom; her poor old heart had given out, and she had died in the orchard among the geese and the fluffy chickens, and the yellow small daffodils. She was an ugly brown pony, who had lived a long time, but her last year had been a very happy one, and she must have slipped away in the spring sunshine dreaming of the grass in the summer meadows and the long warm evenings still to come.

Chapter 8

Now he was five, Adam started at Kilspindie School, the little
grey stone building on the hill, where he was one of twenty-two
pupils taught by Mrs. Aird who had him, as she did all her
pupils, reading and writing fluently before he was six. He
came back for lunch every day which made it a shorter day for
him, although he had to go again in the afternoon. Even so,
Charlotte missed him dreadfully and spent her time trotting
round after me.

Since the terrible gale Mr. and Mrs. Cobb and Magpie
had taken up residence in our coal shed, and although at first we
tried to wean them back to the little green house, we soon gave
up the unequal struggle and cut pigeon holes in the coal cellar
door, and fixed up a ledge outside for them to sun themselves
on. Two families were raised this spring—Princess and Pinky
(Princess turned out to be a cock bird), and Plum and Young
Cobb. Plum was the most beautiful purply colour with a white
head, and Young Cobb was exactly like his father, though he
took a little time to grow into his full beauty.

This summer the pink Ophelia rose first reached up to our
bedroom window, and the early morning was heavy with the
sound of pigeons cooing, as first one, and then another of our
little flock would land with a heavy thud on the window sill
and tap impatiently on the pane for bread. Not content with
this, they soon got on to the top of the window sill, and in no
time were flying heavily into the room, landing plump on our
bed, and walking impatiently up the eiderdown to peck at
our faces, or coo busily among the pillows. Wond, who slept
on the corner of the bed, would curl round in a tight ball,
peering with cross and ignoring eyes at the pigeons who sat

111

preening themselves on her smooth back. Kirsche, more snug inside the sheets, poked out a fox-like black nose, and then withdrew it hastily again.

In May Jemima hatched out a nest of twelve black-red game chicks on which she had been patiently sitting by the bottom pool. Her small brood somewhat puzzled her by the curious way they had of refusing, in spite of all her admonitions, to enter the water at all. We would see her leading them down in a little line across the orchard, purposefully towards the large pool, and although she entered it and quacked and swam about encouragingly herself, none of her strange children would venture so much as a foot inside it. She became discouraged in the end, and her intense pride in them was somewhat tempered by the sad thought that she had hatched out a set of freaks. Apart from this she proved a very good mother and, despite the long hours spent trailing after her, all the chickens grew up splendidly.

Morgan had several baths in the top pool, now that the weather had turned so hot, and seemed to like the water. To Humphrey's disappointment, she would not start to moult, although she was well fed with every possible delicacy. We took her to stay for a weekend on the west coast with Mr. and Mrs. Struthers, who were a little surprised at such a strange weekend visitor, but quite ready to welcome her. Here she sat on a perch among the tulips and white alyssum gazing with bright hawk eyes over the blue waters of Loch Awe, or sat collapsed on my lap, her feet under as if she were completely secure in a nest of her own.

In June we took a house at the sea for the children, and moved there with a large pile of linen and cutlery, books and wet weather games, complete with Wond, Kirsche and Morgan. Our livestock had by now begun to reach alarming proportions when we all went away. However Jimmy Shields was able to feed the hounds, and our nice Mrs. McAlpin, who came up from the cottages below, would be able to cope with Jemima and her brood, the rest of the cocks and hens and the pigeons. Kitty

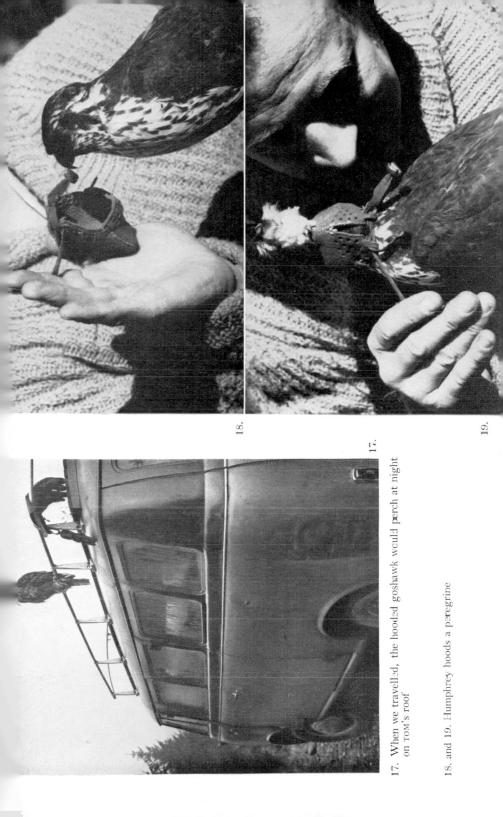

17. When we travelled, the hooded goshawk would perch at night on TOM's roof

18. and 19. Humphrey hoods a peregrine

20. Comfort with her nine puppies: Kingly, Kinsman, Kestrel, Kanute, Kandy, Kentigern, Kindnes Kelinda and Keith

21. Charlotte on Plum, with the young entry

and Goldilocks, Crockett and Plum had plenty of grass in the Dovecote field, now all golden with gorse and broom, besides two running streams full of watercress.

Wond and Kirsche were delighted with the wide sands and the beach, and spent their days running over them, barking at other dogs, and racing like puppies. Wond displayed the same delight as Rheidol had always done in running into the sea half way up her legs, and paddling in it. Kirsche was more inclined to lie back in the sand, hopefully waiting to lick someone's ice cream. Our house was built on the breakwater, literally on the beach, and at high tide the sea came up and lapped the drawing room windows. One of the nicest things about it was the first floor balcony—a great big expanse with railings round it, just above the beach. Here we had most of our meals, on a picnic table, with Morgan watching interestedly from the rail to which we tied her. On 8th June she started moulting; perhaps it was the sea air which brought it on. Once Adam made a giant sand castle for her, with moats and drawbridges and turrets, and on top, sitting on her block perch, was Morgan, gazing at the sea as it swirled nearer round her.

In the middle of the month we took her to stay with some friends for the Highland Show at Ayr. Our friends were becoming used to our turning up with odd hawks and animals, though we never overcame our own surprise at how long-suffering and welcoming other people were. Morgan at least was little trouble, and we left her at night in a cat-free cellar, and by day put her on her perch in a shady part of the garden.

By the time we came back in July Jemima's chickens had grown beyond all recognition, there were two new pigeons in the coal cellar, and the ponies were standing hock deep in sorrel and buttercups. In fact the grass was so long in some places you could scarcely see Plum at all.

A few days after our return when we were beginning to get the sand out of the house, Susan Stirling came over to lunch from Keir with four young kestrels. They were fully feathered and just able to fly: would we like two of them? So Camilla and

Clova joined us. Camilla was larger and pinker, Clova smaller and fluffier—and in spite of their long tails a little smaller than Morgan. Kestrels are a much softer hawk than merlins, their feathers are softer, their colourings more muted, and they fly more like a large moth than with the jewel-like brilliance and precision of a merlin. Strictly speaking, both are long-wings, with brilliant dark eyes, and notched beaks, but in the old falconry calendar while merlins are ladies' hawks, small, deadly and effective, the kestrel is the hawk for the knave, or young boy learning. There is very little you can actually catch with a kestrel, but they do make wonderful pets, and have to be fed as carefully and with the same sort of foods as with any other hawk.

Camilla and Clova were very tame, and we soon had soft leather jesses on them. Humphrey left them largely to Adam and me to look after, and by the end of a week we had them both flying free and regularly to a lure. We released Camilla then, as two hawks were all we really wanted to cope with. We were preparing Goldilocks for Crieff Show, and with the hounds and the garden had little time to spare. For about two or three days Camilla hung round the orchard, coming down for food when she saw us, or when we called her, but then she flew off up the hill towards Evelick. She was a large distinctively pink kestrel, and we saw her several times that summer, and indeed for several years to come, though she rarely came down to our orchard, and never returned to the fist again, even when called and offered choice titbits.

Clova stayed with us all summer, and became a great pet, sleeping in our bedroom on the back of a chair, amusing herself catching moths on the window pane, and even by her presence protecting us from the attentions of the pigeons who banged rudely on the window pane, but did not attempt to come in while she was with us. We took her about in the car with us a great deal, to shows and picnics, and she seemed to like riding about gazing out of the window. Most of the time she was loose, and would come very readily to the fist or lure when called.

Morgan did not care for her, and we were a little careful to keep them apart, as otherwise there might well have been no Clova.

At the beginning of August we had a period of stormy wet weather, and unfortunately on the first day of it Clova hooked off. We were worried about her; we did not think she would be able to fend for herself as readily as Camilla had obviously done, and the rain and cold made a more difficult start for her. We searched the spinney below Kilspindie Quarry, and went up the hill by the Lady's Brig looking for her, and calling her, while the sad August rain dripped on our mackintosh shoulders, and all the Carse below us was shrouded in a driving grey mist. Not a sign of a kestrel did we see. On the third day of Clova's disappearance, the farmer's wife from Newbigging below Errol telephoned.

"We've got a bird in our bathroom which eats bacon and sausages. It seems very tame, and we wondered if it could be yours."

We drove down at once and there, wet and bedraggled, with her feathers very much the worse for wear was Clova. She screamed hysterically and was delighted to see us again, and although she had appreciated the sausage and bacon, was even more pleased with the little bit of raw beef we gave her.

We released Clova about the end of August, and for a long time she lived in the orchard, coming down at least once a day for food, although after a time we could tell she was catching things for herself, for she stopped coming when called, and later took up her abode at the back of Kilspindie Quarry, where we often saw her. She would come and sit in the branches of the apple trees, and look at us with beady kestrel eyes, and once, about two years later, when I suppose she had had a lean period, came swooping through the orchard trees to snatch from Humphrey's hand a small piece of pigeon which he was offering to another hawk. This was the last time we had contact with her, but we still saw her occasionally, and she always looked spruce and well fed.

We had decided to limit our showing efforts to two shows this summer, and had Goldilocks entered in an Anglo-Arab class for both Crieff and Perth. Every evening we groomed and brushed her, and of course Kitty too. Kitty would have to accompany her, for we found difficulty in getting her to lead on a halter. By the time of Crieff Show at the end of July, she looked golden and beautiful, still slightly fluffy, but very sweet.

There was a pink haze of heat over the hills at dawn, and all the grass in the orchard looked heavy and glistening with dew. Humphrey went off early in the horse box with the two ponies, who loaded in very readily, and I followed later with Christian and the two children, Wond and Kirsche and a large picnic basket. It was a perfect day, beautifully hot, and yet with a slight breeze so that we never got too exhausted. The dogs lay panting in the shade of the car, too hot even to make much effort to devour our picnic lunch, the children ate a great many ices, and Adam spent a lot of time marching behind the pipe band in company with a lot of other small boys, Kitty and Goldilocks both looked splendid and Goldilocks came away with a Second Prize ticket in her class.

We were all set to repeat the performance at Perth Show in the beginning of August. However it was not such an unqualified success, and very nearly ended in tragedy. The weather was too hot for one thing, and the show too crowded for another. Kitty and Goldilocks had a small pen between the wall of the showground and the back of the stand, with a narrow muddy lane in front through which all the heavy cattle floats had to pass. We unloaded them nearer the gate of the show ground, and were leading them slowly up this lane towards their pen when Goldilocks suddenly took fright at the loud growls of the Diesel lorry coming behind us. She twisted her halter out of my grasp, set off at a quick canter, shied, reared, jumped in front of the lorry and disappeared underneath it.

I did not know what to do. The lorry was going slowly on, right over the patch of oil and mud where Goldilocks had slipped. There was nothing I could do to save her; I knew she would

116

be squashed absolutely flat by those enormous tyres, churned up by the heavy metal tanks underneath. I turned my head aside and shut my eyes, as the lorry went inexorably on.

"Oh God, why can't it stop?" I shouted to Humphrey.

He handed me Kitty's halter, and I could feel her trembling, her nostrils flaring with sudden fright.

I felt desperately sick.

"It's all right," Humphrey said soothingly. "It's all right, then."

I suddenly opened my eyes, as I realized he was talking to Goldilocks, and not to me. There right in the path of the lorry, her legs tucked under her like a tiny fawn, her head well down, lying crouched to the ground was Goldilocks, black all over with diesel oil and fumes, but miraculously unharmed. It was a miracle.

Humphrey went quietly up to her and got her up by her halter, felt her legs, and ran his hands over her. Apart from the fright, she was absolutely all right. For the next two hours we worked at her, cleaning the oil off her, grooming her, leading her quietly about the show. By the time her class came up for judging she had completely recovered.

They played the theme tune from the film "Round the World in 80 Days" in which Kitty had had a small trotting-on part as a flower-selling pony in the London streets, and she recognized the music, and trotted round in time to it. Goldilocks won Third Prize, and later that evening—much later because there was a hold-up of vans and lorries and we did not get away until after seven o'clock—walked coolly and triumphantly back into the Dovecote Field to tell Crockett and Plum of her experiences. It took us rather longer to recover.

Morgan and Clova both came up with us to stay at Spinningdale with James Robertson Justice, where they were in good company, though we were wary of the peregrines, one of whom was reputed to have killed a merlin a few days before our arrival. After two days successful grouse-hawking with the peregrines, we returned home determined to get Morgan on

117

the go again in spite of her moult. A week later she had a splendid flight after a cock sparrow on the flat field below Kilspindie. Three times she drove him into the hay colls, finally driving him out into the open again and killing him in fine style.

Humphrey fed her up on her sparrow, and brought her home in triumph. However she became very seedy during the night, and put over several undigested bits of sparrow. Humphrey found her looking very poorly in the Mews the next morning, so he dosed her with as much Bismuth Carbonate as would go on a sixpence in a spoon with some Brand's Beef Essence. It was a messy and difficult performance to get her beak open and the medicine inside. We then moved her into the library, and turned the electric heater permanently on. Morgan sat hunched up on her perch, taking little interest in anything.

We had a worrying night with her, and the next day she looked even worse, sitting hunched up in her feathers, eating nothing, her eyes almost permanently shut. Humphrey got M. and B. 693 mixed with penicillin granules from Mr. Macrae which he mixed with sparrows' liver and dosed her with. It was another messy and long-drawn-out job, even though we just had to get about a saltspoonful down. The heater stayed permanently on, and we could only cross our fingers and hope that Morgan would survive.

On the third morning we found Morgan beginning to perk up. Her eyes were much more rounded at the top, and less flat. She roused once or twice while we were there, and accepted a small piece of sparrow with a casting. Two days later she was completely herself again, eating a fresh sparrow morning and evening, and with her recovery the weather changed again, and we had the first sunshine for what seemed like weeks. Morgan came back to the Mews to join Clova, and four days after her illness was in flying order again, and catching food for herself.

It is always surprising how quickly birds can drop off and become ill, or on the other hand, what speed they can use to

118

make their recovery. There seems such a small margin between complete health and the shades of death. Perhaps this speed and lack of stamina is what makes it almost impossible to revive a bird which is in any way run down through lack of food. So many times we have brought in small starving birds in the winter, and only suffered the inevitable heartbreak as we find they are unable to benefit from the food and warmth we can provide.

The weather continued to improve, which was lucky, for we had decided to have one last flight with Morgan, and then gradually hack her back to the wild before the weather broke. It was a heartbreaking decision to make, for we had both come to love her, but her illness had shown us that if we wanted her to survive the winter she must be made to revert to the wild again. We knew we were going to miss her terribly—what other hawk would lie on our bed, or nestle in my lap, would run her beak inside my fingernails looking for any last bits of meat I might have secreted from her? Probably she would not miss us, perhaps she would not even remember: it was up to us how well we did our job of getting her used to the wild again.

Our last flight with Morgan was a warm muggy day; we went out into the marshy fields below Pitroddie, the wide sky turning yellow at the edges like a withering hyacinth, the hay coles misty and dripping with fat drops of dew. Humphrey carried Morgan, ready trimmed for flight, on his fist, and Wond went ahead of us nosing among the damp rushes. Suddenly she froze, almost on a corner, a classic point, her whole body twisted in a curve, her mushroom pink nose barely aquiver. There was certainly something there.

Humphrey released Morgan who was already bobbing her head with ill-concealed excitement. She flew straight up and almost collided with the snipe which Wond flushed a second later from just under her feet. Up and up they flew together until suddenly the snipe broke the tight circling and plunged earthwards. Morgan plunged after her, by some extraordinary

119

fluke or chance struck her, and they came plummeting earthwards together. I do not know who was more amazed, Wond
or Humphrey or Morgan herself. The snipe had no chance
to be anything: it was stone dead. It was a wonderful finish
to our companionship, and obviously Morgan was once more a
merlin in top form.

Humphrey started to put food in the Mews for her without
feeding on the fist. We did not speak to her or make a fuss
of her, and after a week Humphrey removed her bells and jesses,
leash and swivel. He fitted one small silver ring on her leg with
our name and address on it; we didn't want to know if any
terrible mischance befell our dear merlin, but we hoped it might,
like some charm, help to protect her. At first she fluttered
about the orchard, coming back every day to the wall where
Humphrey put food for her. Then one day the food was not taken
and though we kept putting fresh food out, we did not see
Morgan again. She had flown off to her own country, once more
wild and free.

We missed her a great deal, and we wondered a lot: wondered
if she survived the winter, if perhaps by the spring she had
found a mate, nested and reared a whole family of young merlins,
white fluffed and with dark proud eyes.

Having been so successful in hacking back Morgan, we decided
to hack Clova back too. We had to make this decision before
the weather got too cold when it would have been impossible.
Clova was a much more dependent hawk than Morgan had
been. Although she liked the idea of flying free in the orchard,
and even finding her own roosting place at night, she felt that
she needed subsidized feeding. When I came into the orchard,
she would swoop down on me for food, until I had to go indoors
and fetch something. Sometimes for a whole week she would
go off, but she always came back. Swooping low over the orchard
she came to land on my head or arm like a giant butterfly.
Sometimes we would put a fat mouse on the window sill, and
hear a kestrel's wild scream, see the soft flutter of wings as she
swooped past and grabbed it with her feet.

All through that winter Clova continued to hang about, but by the spring we saw less of her, and only once during the next summer did she remember and come diving low into the orchard demanding food. Camilla we still sometimes saw on the hill above Evelick, a large unmistakably pink kestrel, but she remained independent, and took little interest in us.

It was at odd times of the day that I missed our little hawks most: cooking breakfast when there was no hawk there with bright beady eye, waiting for a titbit, or to run her hooked beak along the inside of my fingernail looking for a sucking of egg yolk, or going to bed at night when there was no small kestrel perched headless on the mirror, no merlin nesting like an eider duck on the pillows of the bed.

On the days when Clova came flying back into the orchard for an extra snack, we felt happier, for we knew that for one day at least she did not have to contend with the constant battle for food and existence, which is what life means for a wild animal. But Morgan we never saw, and we thought of her often flying free in the winter skies, swooping and diving, a creature of light, thinking of us not at all.

Chapter 9

WE were not surprised when Christian told us she was going to marry Jimmy Shields, but we were very pleased. The only sad part for us was that they were to live in Paisley. However we cleaned TOM out for the wedding, removing all traces of straw, and tying white ribbons and bunches of white heather all over the front, and Humphrey got a large collection of new pennies to throw to children when he collected Christian from her aunt's house to drive her to the church. Adam and Charlotte were very put out because they had to be clean and tidy for church, and not scrabble about for pennies with the other children. Humphrey gave Christian away, and after the wedding she and Jimmy went off to Paisley in a haze of pink champagne and confetti, very much missed by us all.

Unfortunately we now had no one to leave the hounds with, for our dear red-haired Mrs. McAlpin said she could feed most of our animals, but not hounds, and knowing how savage Rambler could be, I rather agreed with her. Humphrey and I discussed the problem endlessly, for it seemed that if we wanted to keep the hounds on as a pack we would never ever be able to go away together. In the end we made up our minds to disband the pack.

Eric Morrison said he would like to have Rambler and Grayling back to hunt with the Westerby, so that was two hounds settled. We took them to Perth Station and put them on a train going to Rugby; somehow it seemed much longer than a year since we had collected those enormous hounds, and wondered what on earth we were ever to do with them. Now Rambler and Grayling were friends; we could never imagine anyone mixing them up. Rambler I had never got on with, he was too savage and aloof, but I knew that Humphrey was going to miss him desperately. Grayling looked at us with her big Trixie eyes, and for two pins we would have taken them both back home. Only the knowledge that they would be blissful in their own pack made us go through with it at all. We knew quite well that Rambler and Grayling would be so pleased to meet their old friends and biting partners again, that all memory of us would become faint and dim in their minds. But we minded desperately losing them.

Old Garnish with her cracked voice was also surprisingly easy to place, for Mr. Skinner, who lived at Oldwood just below the house, had long coveted her as a guard dog. Mrs. Skinner was never able to housetrain Garnish, so she spent her nights in a kennel in the garden, but she very often managed to break out and we could hear her hunting her way across the fields towards us. Garnish was a complete old reprobate, and nothing would change her habits, but she established a vague friendship with the Skinners, although remaining quite undisciplined. As a guard dog, she was probably excellent. She might have bitten an intruder, and she might not, but at any rate she would have barked in her own individual way.

So we were left with three hounds: Grecian, Lamport and Comfort. We advertised them in the local paper, and a woman with a little girl in Abernethy said she would like Grecian. She was rather surprised when she saw her, and said she had not thought basset hounds so big. However we left Grecian in her clean tidy house giving a fair imitation of a house dog, and kept our fingers crossed that it would be a success. Alas, they only kept her a week, and then they rang up and said the whole house was awash, and they simply couldn't keep her a day longer. Somehow we had known Grecian wouldn't settle; sadly we drove off and brought her back in the van to join Comfort and Lamport in the hound paddock.

The next answer to the advertisement was from two people in Friockheim. We watched them driving up to the door in a bubble car. Humphrey looked at me. "It must be people wanting a basset hound. Which one shall we try them with?"

I said quickly, "Well, we rather like Comfort, and I can see Grecian would hardly be a success in that tiny car; let's try Lamport."

"They couldn't like Lamport, he's so stupid."

However we quickly ran out and brought Lamport into the nursery. His huge clumsy basset paws raced uncertainly over the linoleum.

"I think he looks more at home if I hold him," I said.

We had hardly done this when we heard a knock at the back door. It was the occupants of the bubble car, a tidy looking couple.

"We came about your advertisement for a basset hound."

I held the wriggling rather amazed Lamport out to them. "Would you like this one? He's called Lamport, and he's two years old."

Lamport gave a frenzied leap, and jumped into the woman's arms. His long pink tongue began rapidly licking all over her face.

"He certainly seems to like you," her husband said uncertainly, but I could see from her face that she had already decided Lamport was the dog for her. I was glad that old Grecian was still out in the hound paddock; somehow she didn't look at all the same kind of dog, and I had a sneaking feeling that I didn't want them to see Comfort in case they wanted her. We walked out to the yard, Lamport still being carried, and saw that the little car had green tartan seat covers and a small rug in the back.

"We brought a rug with us in case we came back with a basset hound," the woman said diffidently. Lamport slipped out of her arms into the window ledge at the back, and lay on the tartan rug as if he had lived in tidy cars all his life.

"He has of course always lived in a kennel," Humphrey said.

But Lamport's new owners weren't worried. "We'll soon get him into the way of coming into a house," they said confidently.

Lamport lay stretched out in the back, an expression of complete bliss on his rather stupid face. Somehow he knew that there were to be no more bones snatched from his ready jaws, no more snarling and fights for position; he would never need to slink in the background on gingerly feet to get his dinner, and wait with tongue hanging out while everyone else got fed: from now on he was Number One Dog.

The next day a man telephoned from Montrose about our advertisement. He wanted a basset hound to be a guard dog, he said. He lived just outside the town, and had a nice garden, most suitable for dogs, and he wanted one who would bark at strangers. We assured him that Grecian would almost certainly do that; we didn't add that she would howl at the full moon as well. He came over that afternoon in a decrepit old black car with lots of string and old mackintoshes and gardening papers and boxes in the back. It was a car which lacked the polish and smartness of Lamport's but was more suited, we felt, to Grecian's personality. We liked him, and so did Grecian. She was not a fussy dog and would go with anyone who would feed her. Her new owner rang up the next day to say she was settling down well, and had an enormous appetite. She slept in the kitchen, he told us, and had a grand bark. From Lamport we had photographs and Christmas cards from time to time; he was, his new owners told us, the most beautiful and best loved dog in the whole of Friockheim.

So five of our pack had found new homes for themselves, and we were left with the first, and now the last of them, little Comfort. Humphrey and I looked at her running backwards and forwards in the paddock after Grecian had left her. We looked at each other, and the inevitable happened, as we had long known it would. Comfort came into the kitchen as a house dog.

Not as big and clumsy as Grecian, we managed to housetrain her by tying her close in a basket in the kitchen, only letting her out at set times. No dog likes lying in her own filth, so by the end of the week Comfort was house trained. She had her lapses of course, and was never other than a complete thief, though with time she became a more subtle one.

Poor Kirsche began to have trouble with her back at this time, a thing which happens to dachshunds because of their long spines. For some reason her hind legs became altogether paralysed. Other things were affected too, so we had to keep her in the kitchen at nights. It was warm and she quite enjoyed the company of Comfort; otherwise I felt she might have resented the intrusion of another dog into the household. Although her hind legs were useless, she would run boldly out on her front legs dragging her trailing legs behind. Poor soft little legs, they got terribly scratched and torn being pulled over the gravel, and though we always tried to carry her to the grass she was such an independent dog that she often rushed out when we weren't there, and we would find her poor legs raw and bleeding. We covered them with sticky plaster to try and protect them, but even this was not entirely successful as it was inclined to pull out her hair.

In the meantime we tried every remedy the vet could give us. We took her into the Dog's Hospital in Edinburgh to have her X-rayed, we tried pills and sun-ray treatment and massage. Through it all Kirsche was brave and long suffering, and happy to be alive; though she could no longer wag her tail, we could see from her eyes that she was smiling at us. In the end we tried strychnine pills, which we gave every day, and strangely, these began to have the desired effect. Gradually life returned to her back limbs, and though she never again became the agile active dachshund she used to be, she soon recovered control over her bladder, and was able to stand, if a little unsteadily, on all four legs, and even run with knobbly and knock-kneed hind legs.

At the beginning of September we got another goshawk. This was a Norwegian eyas tiercel, which means a male hawk taken from a nest. He arrived by train in a small cardboard box from a falconer called Tamblyn. When he arrived his primary and secondary feathers and his train were very bedraggled and battered. Fortunately they weren't broken, a disaster for a hawk, and Humphrey brought him into the kitchen and began dipping them into a jug of hot water, which is the best way to restore a bird's feathers to immaculate smoothness. Afterwards he was given half a small chicken and put in the Mews. He weighed one pound twelve ounces.

At first he was unmanageable and bated whenever anyone went in, or when Humphrey was carrying him on his fist. By giving him a diet of washed meat, which has the goodness washed out of it, Humphrey got his weight down to one pound six ounces, and then let it creep up to one pound eight ounces which seemed to suit the hawk well. He never became cosy and friendly as Svenna and Shilloolabeg had been. Humphrey named him Venom, and I thought the name suited him.

Mike and June Woodford, two hawking friends of ours, came to stay with their family on the way south from Spinningdale. We filled the nursery with camp beds and mattresses for their children, and his mother-in-law slept in the car, which she said she preferred. Their well-trained goshawk spent the night with Venom in the Mews, both gazing suspiciously and savagely at each other in that predatory way goshawks have.

"If I weren't tied up with leash and jesses I would make mincemeat of you," said the visiting goshawk.

"If I were only free, there would be nothing left of you," sneered Venom. Savage golden eye sought to outstare savage golden eye, until gradually dusk deepened into night, and only by the slight stir of a foot, the suspicion of a bell's tinkle, did goshawk know that goshawk lurked beside him. They fell silent, dreaming their hatred of each other.

During the next few weeks Humphrey was carrying Venom every day sometimes for four hours at a time. Although he was only a light hawk, nothing like the weight of a female goshawk, Humphrey found it tiring on the fist. When we went to stay with the Stirlings at Invermark in October, they invited Venom as well. It was a good hour's journey in a car from Kilspindie, and I knew only too well about transporting goshawks in cars. Besides, Venom was a mean and tiresome hawk, or at least I thought so.

"Why can't you give him a tranquillizer for the journey?"
I asked Humphrey.

He eventually agreed, and gave Venom a quarter of a tablet
of Equanyl. The poor hawk became terribly drowsy, lurching
about, hardly able to stand. We thought perhaps we had killed him.
However we laid him carefully on a polythene bag on my lap
and set out. On our arrival we were met by Susan Stirling who
offered Venom all possible comforts—a bedroom of his own
in the dry, mounds of clean newspapers, and a dog-free enclosure to perch during the day in company with her own
hawks. He was still very dopey when we arrived but after
half an hour had perked up and was quite ready for the meal
Humphrey gave him. He kept it all down, and seemed to have no
after-effects from the Equanyl. In fact, doping him for travelling
in a confined space was such a success that we repeated it for
the return journey, only this time Venom had to recover in his
own Mews, not nearly such luxurious surroundings for a hawk.

When we got back, the telephone rang about eleven o'clock
at night. We were not unduly alarmed by the lateness of its
ringing, because we knew it would be Walter Joynson. It was.
A keeper near him had trapped a female haggard sparrowhawk
and brought it to him. Walter did not want her at the moment—
would we like her?

I had not taken to Venom much, and was still missing Clova
and Morgan, so I thought it would be nice to have a little hawk
in the house again. A sparrowhawk is very different from a
merlin or a kestrel. It is about the same size certainly, but it is
a short-wing hawk rather than a true falcon, and in many ways like
a miniature goshawk. They have yellow eyes, and long stalk-like
yellow legs. Sparrowhawks are very nervous birds, and get
sudden cramp in their legs caused by a nervous spasm. We
fetched the sparrowhawk over from Kinlochard on our return
from Invermark, and I carried her back sitting on my fist. We
called her Star, and I was at first horrified to find her hanging
limp from my fist with legs which nervelessly refused to
work. However Humphrey explained that this was a charac-

22. Morgan the Merlin breakfasts with us on the terrace at Elie

TWO HOLIDAYS

23. The *Wetter Fugel* anchored in a Friesian canal

24. Megginch becomes a pirate's castle for the day

25. Game chickens by the top pool in Kilspindie garden

teristic of sparrowhawks, and by carefully balancing her back again, and talking in a soothing voice, we managed to get her to sit reasonably on my fist. Star was a dear little bird and came to live in the kitchen straight away, although she never got as tame as Morgan and Clova, and always bated when I offered her titbits.

Soon after her arrival, we went to an Estate course in Galloway, so Humphrey fixed a perch for Venom in the corner of TOM, and we put Star into the cardboard box Venom had arrived in. They travelled well, and while there a gamekeeper let us keep Venom in a disused henhouse, while Star lived in the car. When some of the other people on the course were going surreptitiously to their cars to let out and feed dogs, we were doing the same for our hawks.

On our return Humphrey tried to fly Venom to the lure rather than the fist, which had so far proved a failure, and soon noticed a definite improvement. Venom must have been idle for a long time indeed before we had him, for it was some weeks before we could get him flying to us on a creance. Humphrey had him flying free to the lure on the 24th October, and by the end of the month he caught his first moorhen in the wood below Shipbriggs. Venom struck the moorhen from behind with his hind claw, and they both fell into the stream together, Venom refusing to let go the dead moorhen, and emerging wet but undaunted.

Humphrey decided to imp in some new feathers to replace his broken primaries. This is a complicated process rather like fitting a jigsaw puzzle together. You cut back the old feather and slice a new one to fit joining them with a small piece of wire. This is why all falconers keep their hawk's feathers when they moult, as they may at any time need a replacement. Imping in feathers is only a temporary measure until the new feather can grow in properly.

I had got Star to fly to me on a creance, but had not yet taken the risk of flying her free. In November we went away for a few weeks, and Walter very kindly said he would look after Venom and Star for us. Alas, when we came back we found Star had gone. After two or three free flights she had hooked off, and not been seen again. Walter was very upset, but we consoled him, knowing well how awful we had felt about Shilloolabeg. Venom had apparently got very wild, broken a train feather, and put on weight up to one pound twelve again.

Humphrey started the laborious process of carrying Venom to tame him, and feeding him washed meat again to get his weight down. One day while he was walking up the stream behind the house he suddenly came across a heron who was standing looking remarkably tucked up. Humphrey quickly brought Venom down and put him in the Mews, and called for me. We found we were easily able to catch the heron. He was very emaciated, and had been riddled with shot pellets. We fed him with bread soaked in milk and a little sherry, which was difficult to get in. Humphrey pushed it inside his long beak, while I held him.

"But for goodness sake be careful," Humphrey warned, "because his beak is like a dagger."

We managed to get him to keep some of it down, and the next day went to buy goldfish for him. Adam said he would catch fish in the stream, but after a long time fishing was not successful. The heron did in fact eat two goldfish, but was too ill to be rallied by anything we could do.

"I'm afraid it's no good," Humphrey said as we carefully wrapped him up in a straw nest in the corner of the garage where it was quiet and dark.

We both knew that there was nothing we could do, but we were sad just the same when we came down next morning to find the heron dead.

"I wouldn't even have minded about our trout if I could have had a tame heron," Humphrey said. Even when we found him, it was too late: he had got to that stage from which there is no recall.

Venom's left leg became slightly swollen due to the jess, Humphrey thought, so he removed it and bathed the leg regu-

130

larly with iodine. Venom was by now flying well, and had two
more successful flights at moorhens, one at Shipbriggs and one
at Balcallum.

With all this flying and falling about in water, Venom's
feathers were in a bad way, and Humphrey decided to do some
more imping. Therefore one evening when I was sitting
darning by the fire in the library, he brought Venom in and gave
him a dose of Equanyl. Venom was given the dose at six o'clock,
and by half past eleven was fully doped. Humphrey had all the
feathers laid out on the writing desk, and laid Venom, by
now exceedingly sleepy, on a soft velvet table cover. If we
had not used Equanyl before we should have been extremely
worried. As it was, we had that tiresome hawk under control.
Humphrey imped in five left wing primaries, but did not
touch the right wing since, although six primaries were
broken, they were only broken at the tips and all evenly
so, and his replacement feathers were hardly any better. He
also imped in four train feathers and cut out and replaced a
fifth. By the next morning Venom was back to his usual form,
and looking in much better shape.

Humphrey started hawking again with Venom, and had
two or three days when they could find no moorhens about,
or if they found them could not put them up. The moorhens
ran cunningly scurrying along a bank and lay under tufts of
grass where Venom could not see them. By December he was
being flown at pheasants. The first one was put up by Wond
after an excellent point and flew over the hedge, being closely
pursued by Venom. The other side of the hedge was a field of
turnips and the pheasant plunging into this, Venom became
unsighted and had to be called back. The second pheasant
chased by Venom was at Malcolm's Acre, where Humphrey
released him at a hen pheasant along the side of the woods.
The pheasant had the edge on Venom as far as flying was concerned, and managing to increase the distance, finally disappeared over the trees.

In the next field a moorhen got up which Venom caught, and

Humphrey, encouraged by this success, slipped him at a brown owl, in the hedge. Venom took a poor view of this and sat in a holly tree beside the Pow, until Humphrey approached when he flew off to a pile of brushwood. Humphrey was able to take him up here, and started walking back along the thick ditch which runs up to Annat. Here Venom went pounding through the undergrowth with Wond working well, and took another moorhen at the top. He was not terribly keen to relinquish his prey to Humphrey, and was seen to be quietly slipping off with it. However the dead moorhen was quite heavy, and Venom after all the day's exertions was tired, so Humphrey was able to take him up safely.

Venom's habit of carrying his prey off got worse during the next week or so, and Humphrey found him lurking suspiciously quiet by the side of a stream with a dead moorhen after one flight, hoping he would not be found. Another time when flown at the bottom of the Park at Megginch he disappeared altogether, and was only found by Wond who discovered him sailing down the stream sitting on the back of his prey, silent and unmoving in the hopes that he might escape discovery. However Humphrey waded in after him and picked him up, and he had another two successful flights that same afternoon.

By the beginning of December Venom had moved into the kitchen.

"It's too cold out in the Mews for him," Humphrey said, "and you'll like him better when you see more of him."

Although he was such a splendid hunter, I never did. He had a petty, mean nature, and never liked either of us. I believe all his waking moments were spent in plotting how he could get away, although when they were actually hunting together he retained a certain tolerance for Humphrey.

On Christmas Eve there was a Christmas party in the school. Adam and Charlotte both went to it, and Humphrey left half way through to feed Venom, who he had tied to a fence post on the school playground. He untied the leash and called Venom, standing a few feet away, thinking that Venom would hop those few feet. Venom stood there bobbing his head. It was practically dark and drizzling with a thin cold rain. Suddenly he realized cunningly that he was free, and dashed past Humphrey into a bush. Humphrey got out the lure, appreciating what a hideous mistake he had made, but Venom ignored it, and swooped into the top of the tall ash tree by the waterfall above the mill dam, where he stuck. Humphrey came into the school party and said to me quietly, "Something rather unfortunate has happened. Venom has flown into that ash tree above the mill dam with his leash and swivel on, and got tied up. He's sitting there, and can't get away."

He got Tom and Gordon Logie from Megginch and the three of them carried up ladders from the farm to the mill dam below the school, while I bathed Adam and Charlotte and put them to bed. There was a full moon, and the rain had evaporated into a light mist. Gordon swarmed up the last bit of the ladders, cut Venom's jesses and got him down, holding him squawking and furious under his arm like an old hen while he untied the leash and swivel. Humphrey was waiting for him halfway down, and gave Venom a good feed, and re-jessing him put him in in our warm kitchen. Venom did not at all appreciate these kind attentions. He was furious at being caught, and sat hunched and cross.

The winter was mild and rather wet, and Humphrey did a lot of hawking with Venom.

In February a new goshawk arrived. She was an intermewed passage female, ostensibly for Walter Joynson. She came from Germany, and we were to keep her until Walter was ready for her. She arrived in a minute cardboard box, much smaller than the one Venom had travelled in, in which she had been journeying ever since she left Germany. She was short of a nail on her left foot, and the tips of her train and wings were damaged but otherwise she seemed to be in good order. We took her out gingerly, having become used to the mean characteristics of Venom, and found her bigger, surprisingly tame, and most beautiful. She had a kind, friendly expression in her eye, and we both took to her at once. Walter had been planning to call her Angarschka which means Warrior, but we called her Hesse after her place of origin. She weighed two pounds eight ounces, and she was nicely marked with brown and cream vertical bars.

Hesse came into the kitchen for better manning, and Venom went back to the Mews. I found her a charming companion, twisting her head round backwards in an effort to see what I was doing when I took down cookery books, or peering hunched and greedily at me for titbits like Morgan used to do. I was very cautious at first, remembering how Svenna had used her feet to strike, and how even the nicest looking hawk can be dangerous. Hesse was always charming, and never made any attempt to be savage.

In March Humphrey travelled south to Wales. We still had the two goshawks, Venom and Hesse, and I hoped he would take Venom with him, and leave Hesse with me. However he decided that Hesse was in process of being manned, and would benefit more from the journey. I was used to goshawks by now, and perfectly happy to be left with Venom, so I moved him into the kitchen for warmth, carefully protecting the spice cupboard behind his perch with newspaper. The weather was cold, but not unduly so, and not raining, so the day after Humphrey had gone I put Venom out on his perch on the lawn.

When I went out later in the morning I found him flapping on the ground in the most extraordinary way as if he were having a fit. I couldn't think what to do, however I quickly untied the leash and brought him into the library where there was a fire. He seemed to have altogether lost the use of his legs. I left him on the floor with the door shut to prevent Comfort getting in, and brought in a basin of hot water. I bathed his legs in this until they became more normal; at first they had seemed all stiff, and he kept kicking them as if he had cramp. However after some time feeling seemed to come back to them, so I dried them carefully, and spread some newspapers on the floor as I didn't think I should put him straight on a perch. He seemed stiff and shaken but more or less able to stand on his legs. I gave him a peppercorn wrapped in raw liver, as Humphrey had told me these were good for hawks, and then managed to force a small teaspoon of sherry down his throat. I then shut him in the warm and left him.

Adam came home for lunch, and there were the dogs to feed, hay to put out for the ponies, and the hens waiting for their afternoon wheat, so it must have been about two hours before I was able to get back to Venom. To my horror I found him lying stiff and dead on the floor with his legs scrunched up as if he had had another fit. I felt awful that night when Humphrey telephoned, and I had to tell him the sad news.

However we still had Hesse, who had apparently been a great success with Humphrey. He had taken her to see Bradd, falconer to the late Lord Howard de Walden and had already had her flying free and caught her first rabbit.

"I'll ring up Walter," he said, "and see if he really wants Hesse. There was nothing more you could have done about Venom."

It was a comforting thought, but I was very sorry just the same. Humphrey returned the next day jubilant with Hesse. Walter didn't really want her just now, so we were able to hang on to her. Hesse fluffed and roused and was pleased to come back to her perch in the kitchen.

.   .   .

This year we planned a Robin Hood party for Adam's sixth birthday.

"All bows and arrows, and everybody dressed up," he said.

Kitty was nearly due to foal, so we decided to have no ponies in Sherwood Forest: however we did have a hawk, sitting nicely on her perch. Humphrey thought she would have looked well hooded for the occasion, but Hesse thought otherwise, and shook her head and scratched with her feet until she had got the hood off. Humphrey dressed up in Sherwood green, and all the children arrived in fancy dress, with bows and arrows and hoods, and two of them had sacking wound round their legs with string in an authentic Saxon way. When the children had all arrived,

Humphrey gathered them round him outside the battlemented and turreted front of Megginch to explain the route of their treasure hunt through the forest.

Suddenly he shouted "Look!" and pointed upwards at the battlements.

Everyone turned their faces up to look, and there leaning down sinisterly was a man in a suit of armour.

"One of the Sheriff's men!" Humphrey shouted, and fitting an arrow to his bow, shot it upwards. There was a twang as the arrow connected and then a moment later a thud as the body toppled head first from the roof and hurtled straight through the sky to thud on the ground, the arrow still stuck in it. Humphrey led the children away through the woods before they could inspect the body too closely, for it was in fact made of straw and clothed in a suit of knitted dishcloths painted with aluminium paint and, although riven by the arrow, had in fact been tumbled over by my brother-in-law, who lay in wait behind the battlements ready to push at the strategic moment. However the children went off through the woods before they could see all this, and found Friar Tuck distributing gold coins, a lollipop tree and a magic fish pond. Everybody rather forgot about the body, or at least I thought they had, until some weeks later I met one of the mothers, and she said, "I thought that was a real person falling from the battlements. I got a terrible shock, I thought Humphrey and Cherry have really gone too far this time."

Although Kirsche's legs were by now working more or less normally, she still didn't seem well, and Mr. Macrae said she had gall stones, which would have to be removed. This meant an operation, but she seemed so feeble and unhappy that in the end we decided to have it done. Humphrey and I went with her to the vet's, and it was worse than it had been with Grecian because Kirsche was my own little dog who had been with me always, and she felt that I was betraying her in bringing her there. Knowing how dreadful we had felt on seeing Grecian come out of the anaesthetic, we took care not to go until Mr.

Macrae said she was all right. He had removed a great many gall stones.

"I don't know how the poor doggie got about at all with all that in her," he said.

He didn't hold out any very great hopes of a recovery to us, although Kirsche was only nine, for she had had a long bad winter with her back and now all this. I wrapped her in a blanket I had brought and carried her back on my lap in the car, while Humphrey drove. We made a warm corner for her basket in the kitchen well lined with blankets, and she was terribly pleased to be home again. We carried her outside from time to time during the day, and she was able to stand a little on her legs, but was terribly weak and thin. We could not get her to eat anything, and had to force-feed her with warmed milk and egg which we poured into the side of her mouth with a teaspoon. Sometimes we put a little sherry in it.

She lived for three days, getting gradually weaker in spite of all we could do. But she was happy just to lie in the warm kitchen, and wagged her tail feebly when we came near her or spoke to her. Every night we tucked her up warmly with a hot water bottle, and left a saucer of warm milk and egg beside her, hoping she might lap it. During the night Humphrey or I would come down two or three times, and force a little warm milk inside her. She slept lightly, her breathing so soft she would not have ruffled a daisy in the grass.

"Dear Kirsche," I said, and she opened her eyes and twitched the end of her tail.

On her last night Humphrey and I both felt restless about her. She slept as peacefully as usual. At two o'clock she was sleeping sound and light. When I went down at five she was dead.

I sat in the kitchen a long time and cried, and thought of her as a puppy, thought of her warm black nose, never to sniff and nuzzle into my hand again, thought of the faithful way she followed me about, of how she had taken to Adam and Charlotte and in the end thought of them as overgrown puppies, of how she had slept warm in my bed, or curled in my sewing basket

137

like some golden plush cushion, thought of her warmth and her gentleness, and her sharp white teeth. And now she was dead, and gone from me, gone where spring goes, and the wind, and the falling blossom and the candle flames at night. And all that was left was a poor ill dachshund body already stiff and cold and smelling of death. There would be other dogs, I knew, warm and cuddly and loving and affectionate, and I would probably love them each just as much, but they would not be the same dog, because with Kirsche a whole part of my life had gone too.

I was still sitting at the kitchen table when Humphrey came in. He did not ask about Kirsche, he must already have known.

"We'll need a hot bran mash, with plenty of sugar in it," he said, "and we'll call the new foal Kirsch because he was born the night Kirsche died."

Chapter 10

APRIL is a cold month in Scotland, and one day sitting by the bottom pool Hesse seemed to have caught a chill. Jemima did not care for her there, and the moorhens kept themselves covered among the yellow flag irises. Hesse peered at them with her gleaming eyes; she knew quite well they were there, and could see their shadows flickering on the edge of the water. In the evening when Humphrey came to take Hesse in, she was looking a little off-colour. She cast up part of the fresh pigeon she had been fed on. Humphrey gave her some Bismuth in egg yolk which she lapped avidly off the edge of a coffee spoon. We took her into the kitchen, and kept her there all night. The next day she looked a bit better, but we kept her in for two days more just for safety, and gave her some more Bismuth in egg yolk.

Hesse was quite pleased to be permanently in the kitchen, and followed my every move with the same interest she had shown in the moorhens. She was exceedingly tame, liked being stroked, or having the edges of her neck feathers ruffled with one finger. She did not even mind if I ran my hand over her train, or pushed titbits into the side of her beak. She soon recovered and returned to her apple tree in the garden.

We had made Hesse a beautiful perch on the outstretched branch of an apple tree. We had hung the usual piece of canvas sacking below so she could climb up, and here she sat preening herself among the pink and white apple blossom. Like all hawks, she enjoyed the early morning best, and sat turning her head round enjoying the morning sun. She began to moult in the beginning of May, and although the nights were warmer we still put her inside at night. Even in May you sometimes

139

get a night frost in Scotland, and we did not want to risk her catching another chill. However we moved her out from the kitchen to Venom's old perch in the Mews, and I scrubbed down and disinfected the spice cupboard behind her perch, where the newspaper had not always quite covered it.

One night Hesse bated off her screen, caught her hind claw in a loose thread of sacking, and hung herself in it. Humphrey found her in the morning. We were both speechless with sorrow. We had loved Hesse most of all our goshawks, she had been so cosy and friendly, chirping like a sparrow when we went out to see her in the morning, preening and fluffing herself and peering at you in a conversational way. Only the week before she had been down to the Borders with us on a fishing trip, living on her perch in TOM, cosy and happy, and catching a stoat on the banks of the Tweed, flying with lightning wing beats and steel-tipped claws.

"It's not everyone who comes to fish and catches a stoat," said Mr. Hume the keeper. Hesse was delighted with herself; she had known well enough there was something moving stealthily through the wild garlic.

Humphrey and I blamed ourselves bitterly for not checking to see whether the sacking below the perch needed renewing, for not going to see Hesse after it was dark, for keeping her in the Mews at all.

"She could well have been out on her apple tree."

We knew in our hearts that it was not our fault, that it was a thousand-to-one chance, and that nothing we could do would bring Hesse back, but we minded so much that we felt better blaming ourselves. I could hardly bear to go into the garden, for there on the apple bough was the empty perch, sunlight glinting through the leaves and blossom, and the wild grey goshawk gone for ever.

.   .   .

Three days after Hesse died, we sent the children and Wond to stay with my parents, packed ourselves and Comfort into

TOM and set off for the Hound Show at Aldershot. We were very glad to go, though we kept glancing into the back where there should have been a perch with a goshawk sitting. Above the noise of the engine, like a faulty motor bike, we kept straining our ears for the tinkle of a goshawk's bell, and then remembered too late that there was no goshawk with us any more.

Comfort was delighted at going with us; she sat up on the front seat peering out with bright houndy eyes and looking at the countryside. Since the departure of her friends she had become a complete house dog, watching Wond's example and trying to follow what she did. We had to be careful of her, for she remained thieving and untrustworthy about food she found within reach of her nose. And her nose sometimes jumped on to the table with the rest of her, which made it more difficult. We had entered her for the Show, and Eric Morrison had also entered Rambler and Grayling for us, and was bringing them to the Show. I was greatly looking forward to seeing them both again, and wondered if they would know us and be pleased to see us again.

"You know," I said to Humphrey, "the night that Hesse died the swallows were making an awful noise round our window."

"There was one on top of our window the next morning peering into our room," Humphrey said, "almost as if it had come to tell us something. They are strange birds."

We spent that night camped by a stream near Penrith, sleeping on a mattress in the back of TOM. Driving down was necessarily a leisurely business, because of the paralytic noise, with the result that we didn't like driving for more than two or three hours at a stretch, so as to stop and relax. We had a small bottled-gas stove in the back on which we could boil a kettle and cook up eggs and sausages, which proved immensely useful, for it meant that we were virtually independent, besides being a great deal cheaper. TOM proved quite comfortable to sleep in, although Comfort took charge of the proceedings and slept as near to us as she could.

The next day we spent so much time jaunting about sight-seeing and looking at houses and churches, and all the things which one normally has little time to see that it was after dark when we arrived at Aldershot. Humphrey parked TOM in what looked like a nice convenient wood, and here we undressed and spent a comfortable night under the shelter of the trees.

We were woken soon after five by bugles blowing: we had inadvertently parked the car right in the middle of an army camp. It took us a remarkably short time to get dressed and pack up. We did not feel exactly fresh; however, we found a hotel where we were able to have a wash and tidy up and a large hot breakfast. Comfort had already been brushed and was delighted with the warm rolls we brought out to her. We had brought white coats with us, and Humphrey had a bowler hat. I had wondered whether I also ought to wear a bowler, but Humphrey dissuaded me. As soon as we felt human again we drove to the place where the Show was being held, and found a line of kennels inside tents. From a long large van some of the pedigree Grims bassets were emerging, really beautiful dogs with ears which swept the ground, high domed foreheads and wide splayed feet. We stared at them riveted, and then the Westerby van drove up and among a huge crowd of hounds which poured out we recognized Rambler and Grayling.

"Rambler! Grayling!" we cried ecstatically, but although they turned their heads briefly at the sound of their names, they were not prepared to recognize us. Later when we had separated them from their friends and put them into a large kennel labelled Kilspindie Bassets, they walked round us sniffing in an aloof way, although Grayling jumped up on us. This was probably her natural effusiveness rather than any recognition. Rambler certainly recognized Humphrey, but was not prepared to be demonstrative. They were really more interested in Comfort, walking round and round her with their tails stiffly in the air, Rambler with his hackles bristling, Grayling growling to herself in a soft hum. Comfort growled horribly and showed all her teeth. To us she seemed a perfectly enormous hound, to Rambler and Grayling she was scarcely bigger than a puppy and only half their size.

Stanley, the kennel huntsman from the Westerby, was thrilled to see Comfort again. "There's little Comfort then," he kept saying, and Comfort was overjoyed to see him.

After reintroducing our hounds to each other, and seeing there was not to be an imminent fight, we left them alone to get used to each other, and wandered off to look at some of the other hounds. Several had already escaped their owners, and we had quite a chase all over the Showground to get them back.

Humphrey showed Rambler in the Stallion Dog Hound class; we had been busy brushing him most of the day, and when he walked round with Humphrey I thought he looked very splendid and a credit to the pack. After some discussion among the judges, he was given Second Prize, and his half brother, Westerby Sabre, the First. Sabre was very like Rambler but much lighter in bone. Their father, Westerby Gaelic, who was also there, was a litter brother of Grayling's, and Sabre had the same large Trixie-like eyes that Grayling had. We were terribly pleased when Rambler picked up his blue rosette and felt that our journey had indeed been worthwhile.

I was a little worried about Comfort as all the hounds were so tremendously houndy, and her coat was smooth and sleek like a dog that sleeps warm. Anyone looking at her, I felt, would recognize that smooth sheen that only blankets can give, and also when all the proper kennel hounds were being shown, bits of biscuit were thrown out to them which they ran and scrabbled for in a proper houndy way. Comfort, I knew, was too sophisticated and well fed to run and scrabble for biscuit. However I had the answer to this one, for in the pocket of my white overall, carefully wrapped in a handkerchief, I had a small handful of tinned dog-meat. I felt if I could only throw this instead of biscuit, I might be able to induce Comfort to run across for it.

She was entered in a large class of seventeen, and as we walked round I felt quite nervous and yet exhilarated as I found the numbers thinning out, and Comfort still there. At length the time came when I had to throw my biscuit. Holding my hand with the meat in it a few inches from Comfort's nose I threw it as far as I could, but of course it was inclined to scatter and bits and pieces fell here and there. However Comfort wagged her tail and looked keen, and ran about eating them up. One piece fell among the box of prize rosettes and was missed by Comfort, but the next hound to be exhibited, an engaging curly-coated Griffon Vendéen rather like Garnish, made a beeline for the box, and not only emerged with the dog meat triumphantly eaten, but holding on to a First Prize Rosette. As a result of such splendid determination she was awarded a Second, and Comfort came in Sixth, which I thought was very good.

Grayling was in the Brood Bitch Class, and came away with a yellow Third rosette. Altogether it was a day of fantastic success for us. It was especially nice to see Rambler and Grayling so happy, and we planned to call in on the Westerby Kennels on the way back and leave Comfort to be mated with Rambler, for we felt it would be nice to have basset puppies. In the evening we said goodbye to Rambler and Grayling who scrambled eagerly back into their hound van, while we drove off with Comfort to camp beside a stream.

On the way home we left Comfort at the Westerby Kennels and drove on home without her, but with all our rosettes and prize cards. When we got home we were surprised to find the walls of the passage outside our bedroom splashed with mud and up in the far corner over a window a large swallow's nest had been built. We had fortunately left the window of our bedroom open, and the swallows had flown in, across our bedroom, through the door and up to the corner above the passage window. The mud splashes were caused by building the nest with wet mud which they had carried up from the pool in their beaks. We decided to leave it there, though we did not feel they would continue with it once we were back home. However they did, and by the end of May the first egg had been laid.

26. Zita the peregrine sleeps peacefully in Kilspindie kitchen

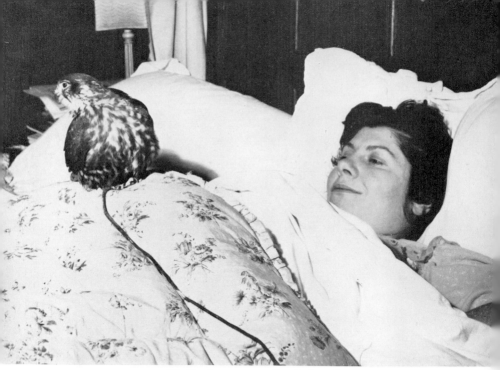

27. Pearly was normally a bed merlin

28. But when Humphrey was born she sat on top of the four-poster

They were due for a little peace and quiet, for although Humphrey was to be there off and on, in June we had again rented a house by the sea in Elie, and I went there, taking Adam and Charlotte with me. Humphrey came backwards and forwards at weekends, bringing Wond with him whenever he could. Pamela Carmichael, a friend of ours, shared the house with us the first fortnight, bringing her two little boys, Alastair and Malcolm, and her plump comfortable nanny, Mrs. Yeaman, who cooked huge meals for us all. It was a time of complete bliss for the children. In the morning they ran along the street barefooted, to buy papers and warm morning rolls from the baker, dabbling their feet in the sea below the window as the fresh bubbly waves of the tide curled back over the satin sands.

We had been there about a week when Humphrey came and told us about the swallows who were beginning to sit. He said they had become acclimatized to him, and did not seem to mind his coming in and out.

Adam and Alastair did a great deal of fishing off the pier, mostly catching saithe, and were thrilled when Humphrey told them he had a boat at St. Andrews which he was going to bring round. Pamela and I decided to give him a hand to sail it round the tip of Fife Ness the next evening.

"But no children," Pamela said. "It might turn cold later, and take some time."

We provided ourselves with sandwiches and left Mrs. Yeaman in charge of the children.

"I've made macaroni cheese for you which I'll put in the oven," she promised.

"And if we're not back by ten o'clock ring up the lifeboat," Pamela said laughingly.

Mrs. Yeaman promised to do that. We drove over to St. Andrews where we found the boat, the *Tangle*, sitting in the harbour. Although the boat was structurally sound, Humphrey had not been able to get the engine to go, and consequently had attached the outboard engine from his Tay coble on the back. She was too big and heavy to row, so this meant that we should be able to get round Fife Ness in two or three hours we thought. We climbed down into the boat and stowed our sandwiches and warm clothes.

I had intended driving the car back to meet the boat at Crail, but Pamela said, "Oh come on, it's a lovely night, why not come with us?"

Humphrey agreed. "We can always fetch the car tomorrow. It'll be a nice evening's sail."

That old sea-dog Wond had decided not to come, and remained at Elie with the children. Humphrey pulled the string to start the outboard, and she started like a dream. Watched by an interested crowd of spectators we chugged cheerfully out of St. Andrews Harbour.

The sun was setting as we sailed out into the bay, the sea glassy smooth with apricot and pink reflections gleaming from it to the pale golden sky behind, while small armadas of fluffy yellow clouds like shoals of haddocks drifted behind the twin towers of St. Regulus and St. Rule, the ruined outlines of the Cathedral, and the black bastion of the old castle. So must it have looked to Mary of Guise's French soldiers sailing up the Forth from Leith, and gazing at the peaceful silhouettes of the town against the evening sky, hearing no sound but the lap of the water at our sides, and the brisk sputtering of the engine, made us feel at one with the past. After a time the sputtering of the engine became a little spasmodic, and finally died into silence altogether. We sat there becalmed, watching the beautiful sunset, feeling at one with nature and the evening.

"I can't imagine what's wrong with it," Humphrey said as he wrestled with the outboard.

We were not seriously worried; it was still warm, the sea like a mill pond, and the view of St. Andrews behind us too beautiful to worry about the engine. Pamela and I handed round sandwiches, which we munched while Humphrey worked. The sun went down, the sky faded to palest yellow, and the evening star came out beside a thin uncertain sickle moon.

The engine started again after twenty minutes, and on we

went. It was not dark for there was light from the moon, and still that half light whereby you cannot quite see colours. Someone standing on the quay at St. Andrews had told us something about going round the outside of the North Carr Lightship because of hidden rocks. But we felt safer nearer to the shore with our dicky engine. We went on steadily for another three quarters of an hour or so when the engine gave an apologetic splutter and died on us again.

"I think the trouble is the engine is water cooled," Humphrey explained, "and we're not heavy enough to keep it in the water all the time. It's screwed too high on to the boat."

We got out the oars this time and tried rowing, but the boat was too heavy, and Pamela and I, who held one oar, kept tripping each other up and falling into the bottom of the boat. We became weak with laughing, and stowed the oars, waiting for the engine to cool. About twenty minutes later we were able to start her again—though this time the starting rope broke as it was rotten, and Humphrey had to use shorter and shorter bits as it all broke off in his hand. While we were waiting the moon went down and it became dark, for the wind also got up and the waves became choppy. We finished the sandwiches, after some discussion as to whether we should keep them for when we were swept away into the North Sea and eat them slowly lasting us for days and days, and put on every stitch of clothing we had brought with us. It was cold now, and dark, and there seemed to be some kind of current or tide race. The North Carr Lightship was a long way to our east, the shoreline a dim suggestion of further blackness on our starboard bow.

"Hurray!" Humphrey said as he started the engine by pulling on the minute piece of rotten string which was all that was left. She sounded faultless this time. We all sat in the stern of the boat in order to keep the engine in the water. The noise of the engine was different when she came out of the water from when she went in, a sort of gurgling suck. It took about twenty minutes or a little more to cool down every time it seized up, and presumably if we could only keep it going, and kept it cool we should be able to make our way round the point of Fife Ness and into Crail Harbour. We had abandoned all thoughts of reaching Elie Harbour that night.

The rising wind had driven thick clouds across the sky, so the stars were hidden, and without the moon there was little light. Bumping and bucketing we sailed onwards, eyes strained for hidden rocks. Suddenly we saw ahead a line of blackness more intense than the night, thicker than the waves which rose above us. There was a complete wall of rocks ahead, foam tipped and curled on them, there were rocks on our either side, and then the boat shot high in the air for one awful moment, and went crunch, bang, crunch, bang as it bounded over two rocks beneath us.

They hadn't torn a large hole in the bottom of the boat, it is true, but they certainly made a split in the planking. Pamela and I began to bale furiously. At the same time the engine gave a final disgusted splutter and died away. Humphrey started work at it again, meantime steadying us with the oars. We did not know quite how much damage had been done by the rock, but at least we could see the shore line dimly in the distance. Pamela and I discussed whether we would be able to swim to it, or should we perhaps abandon boat.

"I don't think we've got to that yet," Humphrey said. "It's only a matter of time till the outboard cools down, and then we'll be in Crail Harbour." He was so cheerful and matter of fact that we did not have time to feel frightened, though I could certainly have done with even a chink of starlight, and the sea a little quieter. There were rocks all round us where we were, and the black walls of the waves which swept on us looked nearly as solid. We found a small torch belonging to Adam, but it was not much use in the immensity of blackness.

Time passed and still the engine would not start. It was long after twenty minutes since it had last stopped. Also the breeze was freshening a bit, and the waves seemed bigger. The boat seemed a great deal wetter in spite of the baling. Suddenly in the distance we saw a beautiful rocket shoot into the sky, with

148

green and red stars, and then a few minutes later, an answering one from the south. For a few brief moments the sky was ablaze with glittering stars.

"I don't suppose Mrs. Yeaman did call the life boat out," Pamela said.

"Or that they could be looking for us," I added.

And now from the blackness ahead a beam shot out, and there in the distance was a lifeboat with a big searchlight beam scanning the sea in front of her.

"It won't pick us up, the beam won't go that far, and we can't attract attention," Pamela said.

Frantically we waved our tiny torch, but the beam swept backwards and forwards on a north-easterly line, seeming to ignore us. Suddenly the beam swept over us, we were in the light. We held our breath, waving the torch wildly, hoping they had seen us.

They had. The lifeboat came bearing down on us like a tubby porpoise, lights beaming and flashing. When they were quite close they threw Humphrey a rope. He caught it and made it fast, and then helped Pamela and me on to the lifeboat.

"I'll stay here, if you'll give me a tow," he said.

I felt curiously stiff and weak at the knees when I stepped on to the lifeboat. There was a half covered cabin, and lots of nice cheerful people standing round in yellow oilskins.

"You're lucky," they told us. "Picked a couple of stiffs off these rocks only last week. They're murder. You should have gone round the North Carr Lightship."

We explained about the outboard motor seizing up, and they said, "Would you like some hot soup?"

We thought we would, and they had beautiful big tins which they lit fuses in the top and the tins heated themselves automatically. The soup was delicious, rather like oxtail, and the lifeboat men hauled Humphrey and the *Tangle* in nearer and then passed some soup down to him. Then we all had rum, which was very warming and nice, and after that we felt a lot hotter and braver than we had before. We steamed cheerfully into Anstruther

Harbour soon after four in the morning; already there was a pink tinge to the back of the sky, and colour was beginning to flow through to the pebbles and the greyness at the edge of the harbour. We felt infinitely grateful to the lifeboatmen, and even more so when the coxswain lent us his own car to drive back to Elie.

Mrs. Yeaman met us at the door with her knitting in her hands, she had been drinking tea and tranquillizers in equal quantities for the last six hours. She had promised to ring for the lifeboat at ten when we weren't back, and then we hadn't been. For two hours she could not make up her mind, and finally just before one in the morning she had done that. The lifeboat people had been ringing her back every quarter of an hour ever since; at two the lifeboat definitely decided to go out, and at half past two the first rocket went up and the lifeboat was launched. We felt extremely lucky, and immensely grateful to the lifeboatmen and Mrs. Yeaman, who had probably between them saved our lives.

Exhausted by it all, we tumbled into bed, quite forgetting about the macaroni cheese which had been quietly burning in the oven for the last eight hours.

The day after our lifeboat adventure we spent driving over Fife, returning the coxswain's car to Anstruther, and collecting our own from St. Andrews. The *Tangle*, which was now drawn up on the shingle at the side of Anstruther Harbour, appeared to have two holes in her, but not so serious that they could not be put right. General opinion from the old salts sitting round the harbour at Anstruther was that we had been exceedingly lucky.

Humphrey and I hoped that the luck was going to last, because we had a curious feeling we might be going to need it. The next day we were going to fly down to the wedding of Joshua Rowley and Celia Monckton in Yorkshire. At the time it had seemed the obvious solution to our transport problems.

"How are we to get there and back from Elie?" I had asked. "It'll take two days by train, and it's a frightful drive."

"We'll go by air from Scone of course," Humphrey said. "I can fly you direct to wherever the nearest place is, and get them to send a car for us there."

"Of course," I had agreed. "That would be much easier."

Now I was beginning to have my doubts. If sailing a small boat from St. Andrews round the point of Fife Ness ended in such near-disaster, what would happen when we flew a small aeroplane from Scone to the south of Yorkshire?

"Who is going to do the navigating?" I asked Humphrey, now thoroughly unsure of the whole enterprise.

"You are," he said.

I said, "Oh." There is a saying in our family which came to mind very forcibly just then. Years ago my father saw an old Carse farmer standing looking at his crop of oats which had just been crushed absolutely flat by a gale—it was all lying green and broken with the weeds growing up through it. The old man was just standing there shaking his head, and saying out loud, "So that's to be a failure too." It was a phrase which brought to mind what grandiose visions of disaster and ill luck, the ultimate in pessimism. I thought about my map reading, about short cuts I had advised, ending in grassy hillsides, or deep fords.

I said, "Yes," musingly.

"Well, there isn't time to drive down now or go by train," Humphrey said. "We'd be too late for the wedding."

Pamela had forebodings about our trip too. "I'll look after the children till you get back," she said. She obviously meant "If you don't . . ."

"And we'll wave when we fly over Elie," Humphrey promised. We had an early bed that night, still dreaming of waves and rocks and lifeboat soup, and the next morning Humphrey and I got up in our smart wedding clothes and left the house at eight.

We drove cheerfully northwards to Scone Aerodrome, and were there soon after nine. It was a beautiful morning, the sky new-washed like a hedge sparrow's egg, the hedges pearly with dew and hung with spiders' diamond necklaces. All the birds were singing, and we felt extremely happy.

Pooch Nugent, who runs the Aerodrome, was as bright and early as we were. He had maps of all kinds spread out, and started to show us exactly our route, what compass bearing we were to follow, at what times we should be in what places, and how to refuel at Newcastle. I felt far too optimistic and light-hearted to listen very much; I longed to jump into the aeroplane, and drive off. However I tried to concentrate on the maps and the directions, and Humphrey talked knowledgeably about wind speeds and weather forecasts. There might be some fog drifting in from the North Sea, otherwise the weather was fine. We telephoned the aerodrome at Netherthorpe to check if it was all right to land there, and the person who answered the telephone said it was. We wrote down the radio code for calling Dishforth, a big service aerodrome on the way down, and then we went over the route and the compass bearings once more. I was terribly impatient.

At last, at last, we were in the aeroplane, a small Auster, and Humphrey was checking the controls, the petrol and a great row of little dials which meant nothing to me at all. He showed me the compass, how to set it, and how to work it. I had never been in a small aeroplane before, but had complete confidence in Humphrey's driving. Pooch Nugent's directions about how to find the way seemed very simple, and I was sure I could work the compass bearing. We taxied along the runway, and then Humphrey checked all the contols and the engine. Everything seemed to be in splendid order. Humphrey had put on gym shoes, and put his tidy wedding shoes in the back with his hat. I took my shoes off for comfort, but kept my hat on.

We were running down the runway into the wind, our wheels suddenly clear of the ground, and then we were mounting, turning until the control tower was tiny below us. Up into the blue sky we climbed and then veered south-south-east on our compass bearing, flying low over the green Sidlaws, over the grey ribbon of the Tay, and now Fife lay below us, and there in the distance was Elie a cluster of houses on the shores of the Forth.

We dropped height a little and flew low over the house. Pamela and Mrs. Yeaman and the children were all waving bathing towels at us in the garden. We leant out of the aeroplane and waved back. In no time we were over the harbour, southwards across the wide Firth of Forth, heading for the Bass Rock, and peering down I could see two small fields of potatoes in blossom, grown in a little crevice near the top by the lighthouse men.

It was a glorious day, sunny and delicious, and we both felt extremely light-hearted. As we flew southwards we came to the Border Cheviots, and now vast expanses of bleaker moorland lay beneath us. The weather deteriorated, and in no time at all we were wrapped in a thick blanket of impenetrable fog. We could see nothing; above the noise of the aeroplane engine we could hear nothing either.

"We have to find Newcastle to refuel," Humphrey said. He sounded worried.

"Oh that's all right," I said cheerfully. "I went through all the directions very plainly with Pooch Nugent. You only have to follow this compass bearing and we'll get there all right."

I was supremely confident.

Humphrey confided to me afterwards that he had been in two minds whether to go on or turn back. We were flying blind, entirely reliant on a compass reading of mine, which might be accurate and on the other hand might not. For all he knew we might be flying off at a tangent over the North Sea; we might go on flying and flying in the fog until we ran out of petrol, which would certainly be before we reached Denmark the other side. The compass was presumably accurate and in good order, but I had never worked one before; there was a more than even chance that I might be doing it wrong. Humphrey took the chance. He went on.

We went on a long time. The fog was thick and dense and shrouding all round us, and when we came out of it like low clouds we were over miles of desolate moorland, with no house in sight. I tried to calculate where we were. We had left Scone at 10.40; when we crossed over Elie, it had been one minute past eleven, and it had taken us ten minutes to cross the Forth. At 11.29 we had been over Berwick-on-Tweed. That was nearly half an hour ago. We should have been over Newcastle by now.

Looking up from my calculations I met Humphrey's eye. "Humphrey, I've lost Newcastle," I said desperately.

"Nonsense," Humphrey retorted. "It's a huge town, you can't have."

Just then the fog lifted a little and we saw some houses stretching away to our east. We had found Newcastle, and my compass readings had not been all that wrong. We found the airport, and circled round to land. Taking off had been fun; landing terrified me, I began to go white in the face and clutched my handbag. We lost speed very rapidly and were just coming in to land when Humphrey said, "I wonder if we should land on the grass or the tarmac," and shot up again.

I was so frightened I was trembling all over. To think that we had to do that all over again.

"Oh the grass, I should think," I said with my teeth chattering. It seemed to me it would be softer to fall on if the areoplane nose-dived.

Humphrey circled round and started to come in once more. I shut my eyes and clenched my teeth. We must be nearly landing now, I thought. Suddenly there was a jerk and the aeroplane shot upwards again.

"Don't look now, but there's someone behind us," Humphrey said. We shot skywards just out of the path of a vast airliner which thundered downwards on to the tarmac.

We landed at the third attempt; by that time I was in a state of near-hysteria. It was twenty-five minutes past twelve. We taxied over to the petrol pump and filled up our tanks. What with the delays and everything else, I knew fatalistically and hopelessly that we were going to miss the wedding. There was to be a car meeting us at Netherthorpe at one o'clock to take us back to Serlby for lunch before the wedding at half past two.

But now it was Humphrey's turn to be dogged and optimistic. "We'll just go on and turn up when we can," he said. "Now we've got so far we're not going back."

We filled up with petrol as quickly as we could, paid our three-shilling landing fee (it would have been much more expensive to land on the tarmac, we discovered) and set off again. There was no more fog, and the whole thing would have been plain flying. As we flew past Dishforth, we tried to talk to them, on their frequency of 121.5, but nothing happened. We could hear them talking and talking away, but they either could not hear us or would not answer us.

"So a fat lot of use that would be in an emergency," Humphrey remarked.

We flew steadily onwards. "Now," I said, gazing at the map and peering out of the window, "Netherthorpe should be somewhere here, in fact just there."

We both gazed out but could see nothing resembling an aerodrome at all. There were fields and trees, a canal and a railway bridge, but no sign of a windsock, a control tower or hangars, or indeed any of the things one associates with aerodromes.

"But it must be just here," I said. "Look, that's where it says in the map, and that's that road there. It's just here."

We peered below us, and then as we banked and came in lower, we noticed a brownish thing flying in a field, which could have been a windsock. We saw a hangar to our left, but nothing else. Netherthorpe Aerodrome was nothing more than a medium-sized field.

Humphrey brought the aeroplane round and down and we landed at one attempt without much bumping on the rough grass. I had my eyes shut so tight I didn't see, but it certainly felt much better than I had anticipated. By this time, it was 2.10, and the car must long have gone. We climbed out of the aeroplane, Humphrey jumping down first, then I handed him his shoes and hat, and he helped me out.

We had twenty minutes to get to Serlby, about eight miles away. Without a car it was certainly going to be difficult. We could see about the aeroplane when we came back, we felt. The hangar was shut and no sign of anyone in it. Obviously the place belonged to some flying club, and it was pure chance that the telephone in it had been answered that morning. I ran after Humphrey, clutching my bag, and putting my shoes on as I went. As we got near the high unkempt hedge we saw a car coming slowly down the lane. Humphrey vaulted over the gate waving and shouting and I came up to the gate and went through it just as the car stopped. Of the car which was to meet us there was no sign. However this car turned out to be driven by a Welsh Baptist out on a jaunt.

"When I saw the aeroplane coming down out of the sky and you running down the road at me, it's robbers I thought you were," he remarked, "but then I saw your lady in her hat and shoes, and I wondered whatever you were doing."

Humphrey explained quickly to him about the wedding, and the aeroplane being delayed, and the car not here, and how little time we had.

"I'm partial to a wedding myself," he said, "And as it's my half day and your lady with her hat on and all, I'll drive you there."

So we climbed into his black Ford Popular and set off. Humphrey and I were in a fever to get there, but he was not a driver to be hurried. At every cross roads he stopped some yards before, and then edged forward peering out. At the same time he had discovered that Humphrey spoke Welsh, and a long and apparently violent conversation ensued. However we made it, we got to Serlby. We burst in to the chapel just before Celia did, pushing our way through the guests waiting outside, for the chapel was very small and only held a hundred people, and we had seats reserved for us. We saw Joshua turning round wondering who on earth could be bursting in so late and if it was some last-minute objection—however he saw who it was and waved.

We had made it, we had made it, I thought triumphantly to myself. The service was a beautiful one, the chapel tiny and perfect, and Celia looked lovely. Afterwards there was a huge marquee on the lawn, flowers everywhere, and I drank a great deal of champagne because after all I wasn't driving. Humphrey was rather abstemious.

After it was all over, and Joshua and Celia had driven off in a whirl of confetti, Martin and Toodie Fortescue said they could come with us to see us off.

"I know about aeroplanes from being in the Navy," Martin said, "and I'll come and wind your propellers for you."

We accepted their offer gratefully, but when once in the car had considerable difficulty in remembering where Netherthorpe actually was. We drove round the countryside for what seemed a very long time. At last we found the place, and recognized the gate. However when we stopped the car and peered over it, all we could see was a large herd of cows. The aeroplane seemed to have entirely disappeared.

"Oh no!" I exclaimed. "Look, Humphrey, the cows are eating it!"

"You didn't say there were cows," Martin remarked. "It's a well known thing, they love aeroplanes."

We all went into the field and began to wave our arms about, shouting, "Shoo shoo!" and "Ho!" and "Hoi!" depending from which part of the country we came from. The cows dispersed reluctantly and we went forward to inspect the damage. There were several large holes in the fabric of the aeroplane.

"What shall we do?" I said.

Humphrey and Martin went into the hangar to telephone Scone to tell them what had happened, leaving Toodie and me to drive off the cows. After a bit they came back.

"What did they say?"

"Well, they laughed so much they couldn't say anything for a long time, but when they could they said it was up to me if I thought it was airworthy or not, and to try sticky tape. They said we don't want all our aeroplanes eaten by cows."

Martin and Humphrey went off to the farmhouse to see if they could find any sticky tape, and by good chance were given a large roll of Elastoplast with which we filled up the worst gaps.

"Why don't you come back with us?" Toodie asked me.

"No, I expect it'll be all right," I said, though I had doubts about it.

"Goodness, I think you're brave," Toodie said pressing a large tin of acid drops into my hand.

That was one thing I was not, I reflected as I strapped myself in and removed my shoes. Martin went round to the front of the aeroplane and began to wind the propeller, and we soon got it started.

"I'm going to drive round the field first to chase the cows off," Humphrey shouted across to me. "Otherwise we'll never get a clear space to take off."

We taxied round the field with a cavorting galloping snorting herd of cows prancing and kicking in front of us. Martin and Toodie said afterwards that it was the funniest sight they ever saw. Then when we had a reasonably cow-free space Humphrey turned the aeroplane into the wind and made a run at it. We were off, but there was a large three-foot dip in the middle of the field we hadn't noticed so came bang down again, and then had to really climb very steeply when we actually took off to avoid scraping the slates of the farmhouse roof with our wheels. It was a near thing, and I must have eaten half Toodie's box of acid drops in those first two minutes, I was so frightened.

Once we were airborne, it was all right. We took off at half past seven, and were flying into a strong head wind which not only restricted our speed, but also meant we were using more petrol to go a shorter distance. By 8.17 we had 8 gallons in the port tank; by 8.30 it was only seven; by 8.39 it was six. It was beginning to get dark, and if only Netherthorpe had been the sort of aerodrome you can refuel at, as we had planned, we would

158

have felt a lot happier. As we neared Newcastle dusk was closing in.

"I don't know if we have lights or not, but all the same I think it would be safer to spend the night here," Humphrey said.

We landed at Newcastle at ten past nine, and I have never felt more relieved about anything. By this time we realized that we had very little money on us; however the people in the airport club lent us some money, and Humphrey was able to buy beer and sandwiches and hard boiled eggs. I was long past eating anything, but had a strong brandy and soda which made my knees feel a little less weak.

They offered to put us up—"Just for the night, so you can start first thing tomorrow morning. It's not up to much," they said.

Anything for a bed, I felt. Humphrey rang up Pamela in Elie to explain what had happened.

"I knew you'd land up in some adventure," she said cheerfully, when she had stopped laughing about the cows.

The beds were hard but clean, and I took off my dress and slept in my petticoat. In the morning one of the ground staff came in with a can of hot sweet tea with milk in it and a packet of biscuits from the canteen. He thought it a great joke to see us there.

"First time I've had to bring anything to eat to the people in here," he said.

It was only then that we realized we had spent the night in the mortuary.

It was a fresh glorious morning, the sky rosy and pearly, and we were soon dressed and out to fill the aeroplane up with petrol. Then we took off and soared into the rosy pink sky of morning. We were over Elie by 9.44 and saw WELCOME written with shells on the newly washed beach, and towels laid out in in the garden. We waved frantically, and everyone below waved too.

"See you for lunch!" we shouted.

And we did.

Chapter 11

WHEN we came back from Elie to Kilspindie six baby swallows had hatched out in the nest in our bedroom passage. We did not look at them, but the parents came back and forwards with complete freedom. First one adult bird alighted on top of our window, a light frill of flies round his mouth proclaiming that he was laden with food for the babies. Turning his head from side to side he would survey us and the room, and then fly across and perch on top of the door beside our bed. Then, repeating the same performance, he would fly through to the babies, and we would hear their rapturous cries as food was pushed into them. Then the parent bird would fly round the corner of the door, across our bedroom and out of the window.

They seemed to have a definite feeding pattern. Meals started as soon as it was light, about five in the morning, and for the next hour went on continuously, first one parent bird and then the other. From about half past six till half past eight there was a pause in swallow feeding. Presumably the parents were feeding themselves then, and drinking and resting waiting for the next bout.

But we were not left in peace, for as soon as the swallows had cooled off there was a thud and bang on the window sill, and Mr. and Mrs. Cobb and Pink and Pansy, their new babies, flumped down on the window, puffed themselves out and walked along the top peering in at us, and preening themselves. If the bottom of the window were open they hopped through and walked importantly over all the papers on my desk, ruffling through them with heavy pigeon feet.

From there it was but a short flight to the bed, and there most sunny mornings we would find them, strolling insouciantly over Wond and Comfort, climbing up and down our eiderdown, and demanding food so insistently that we took to bringing something up for them last thing at night.

One day when the baby swallows were well feathered, Humphrey and I got a chair and stood up beside the nest. The parents were away in one of their non-feeding periods, and we cautiously reached up and lifted out a minute dark blue feathered baby. Bright swallow eyes gazed at us unblinking, and then the stumpy-tailed thing shot out of Humphrey's hand to crash land on our eiderdown. Up above in the nest five indignant brothers and sisters shouted their fury at being left behind, and two of them came crashing down from the nest to flap and flap about in our room. We had the most frantic job catching them all and putting them back. Now we realized that they were all but ready to fly. Having carefully balanced them in their nest, which was by now much too small for them all, we tiptoed carefully away, hoping they would not come out again.

A few days later we heard the parents make a different kind of noise when they came in with food. Normally they had a high "Here's-food—come-and-get-it" call. Now the twittering was faster and more urgent, a different sound altogether. We wondered what it was, but as first one and then another short-tailed baby swallow came hurtling into our room, crash landing on the edge of the bed, and the chairs, we were not long in doubt. It was the flying call.

It took the baby swallows three days to learn to fly; the first day they just did circuits and bumps in our bedroom, the second day they were venturing outside. The third day, though handicapped by the lack of feathers, they were flying really quite well. For some weeks after this they continued to sleep in the nest, and then gradually, a few at a time, they went out and roosted under the eaves and in the farm buildings with the older swallows. We felt very proud of our six babies, almost as if we had reared them ourselves.

With the grey wagtail babies we were not so lucky. A grey wagtail had nested in the wall beside the stream in our orchard, and then deserted, leaving four featherless fledglings in the nest. We brought them in, all cold and shivering, and already far gone, and wrapped them in a box in a bit of old blanket above the heater. We managed to catch quite a few flies to feed them, but the experiment was not a success, and they all died. We felt they had been really too young to rear successfully.

At the beginning of August I spent a few days with my parents at Megginch while Humphrey was in London, taking Adam and Charlotte with me, and of course Wond and Comfort. Our dear basset was very definitely in pup now, in fact she was enormous, and I made a nice straw kennel for her in the turret over the front door where Plum had been stabled. The puppies were obviously imminent, so I kept her there at nights in case she started getting ideas about beds and sofas. I had seen her several times looking meaningly at the one in the drawing room, and trying to draw her huge self up on it.

On the morning of 5th August I came down to let her out, and found eight beautiful puppies. I gave her some warm milk and sugar and went to have breakfast with the children. After breakfast two more puppies had been born, but one was dead, a huge beautiful gold and white dog puppy. However nine was as much as any mother could manage. Comfort was terribly pleased with herself. The father was not Rambler as we had hoped, because there had been a little difficulty with him and Comfort, but his half brother Sabre, who had been champion hound at the Aldershot Show.

The puppies were all quite beautiful, we thought. Two of them were lemon and white, a small bitch called Kindness, and a little dog puppy called Kestrel. The others were predominantly black and white or tricolour, with a large quantity of white on them. There was one other bitch whom we called Kelinda. The six other dog puppies were called Keith, Kandy, Kanute, Kentigern, Kingly and Kinsman. Kingly was practically all white, very like Rambler, and Kinsman mostly black with a little white and tan on him. These were the two biggest puppies by a long way. I liked Kingly best, and I think Humphrey liked Kinsman.

When we moved back to Kilspindie we put them all into the hound paddock, but they spent a lot of time in the garden with us, rolling and biting over the lawn, gambolling under Plum's feet, and padding through the house with huge uncertain basset feet. One night we tried taking them all to bed with us but it was not an entire success. Adam and Charlotte loved them, and spent a lot of time playing with them. There was a low iron gate between the hound paddock and the garden, and Comfort, who soon got her figure back, was not slow in learning to jump over this. When the puppies were first being weaned, she would jump out of her enclosure, come into the kitchen, and make a huge meal, wolfed down in a second. Then she would go back to the puppies, jump the gate and sick it all up for them. I have heard of lions doing this, but never dogs. The puppies obviously knew what was going to happen, for they stood in an expectant circle round the gate, waiting for their mother to come back. It felt lovely to have a pack of basset hounds in the hound kennel again.

I felt somehow it would not be long before we again had a hawk. I was right. A fortnight after the puppies were born, Humphrey heard his South American hawk was arriving at Prestwick on a Pan-American aeroplane. He had written to Sterling Bunnell, the American falconer, asking what kind of hawk he suggested would be best for catching hares, and Sterling Bunnell had written back that the hawk to have was a Peruvian falcon called a micrastur semi-torquatus. He had then heard of one who came from Lima, a bird called Chiqita, and this was the one who was arriving at Prestwick.

Humphrey drove over to Prestwick in a state of great excitement, he was going to pick her up in her box and bring her home to jess and bell. We took the crate as usual into the darkened Mews, and were dismayed when Chiqita emerged from her box, for although about the same size as a goshawk, she was a very curious looking bird indeed, not resembling any kind of hawk we had seen. She was dark chocolate brown all over with a creamy ruff and front, dark head and small dark half collar (the semi-torquatus of her name). She had a brown and cream horizontal barred tail, rather pretty, and always stood crouched and peering. Svenna was inclined to be moody and sharp tempered, Venom was mean and could be tiresome; but of all the birds we have ever had Chiqita was the only one who was thoroughly bad all through. Sometimes she could be beautiful; she was always vicious, nasty and evil.

When we got her, she was a choosy and difficult feeder, and in heavy moult, many of her feathers having come out, and not all grown in again. For some reason never entirely clear, we changed her name from Chiqita to Itza. I think we felt Chiqita was a charming gay little name unsuited to her sombre brooding temperament. She gave Humphrey a nasty slash with her talons when he was jessing her. I was holding her upside down at the moment, and thought I had got control of her. Evidently I had not. She quite liked sitting in the garden by the top pool on the goshawks' bow perch, and seemed to take a keen interest in the game birds.

We found her lying down behind an apple tree one day, and Humphrey wondered if the jesses weren't too tight, or her legs sore, but this did not seem to be the case.

"I wonder why she lies down," he said. "She is a very curious bird. It can't be because she finds it too hot here."

We were soon to know. Lying micrastur-o in the long grass she was practically invisible. An unwary game hen walking too close round the apple tree found a scrawny claw stuck into her. There was a frightful screaming scene, and when Humphrey rushed out to rescue the hen it was already too late, and she had to be despatched. I never liked Itza after that. I was too frightened for Jemima, or one of the puppies.

The day after Itza arrived we went over to Keir, and Susan Stirling very kindly gave us a small sparrowhawk. It was a male, and very sweet, much less inclined to hang upside down with rigid legs than Star had been, and we called him Speckle.

He sat quite cheerfully on my ungloved hand, and was soon flying well to a creance.

At the beginning of September my mother had arranged a three-day treat for us all at the Edinburgh Festival. We were to stay in a hotel, leaving the children and dogs behind at Megginch. The only trouble was that the hawks would have to come too. Fortunately Humphrey has a cousin who lives in Edinburgh in a house with a large garden, and he very kindly said we could accommodate both our hawks there for the whole visit. We were immensely relieved about this. We were to drive to Edinburgh in my mother's Mini while the rest of the party would meet us there. Humphrey drove, and I sat beside him holding Speckle in my lap. Itza sat malevolently in solitary splendour on a perch in the back.

As we were coming down the hill towards the Forth Humphrey had to brake suddenly. There was a rush as the front seats tipped forwards, and far worse, Itza's perch was thrown forwards, and Itza herself embedded her talons in the back of Humphrey's neck. I managed to get them out, which was difficult with one hand, because of holding Speckle with the other. Speckle was distinctly alarmed by the whole process and kept trying to bate off to the floor. Humphrey was in agony, and the only person who was enjoying the situation was that horrid Itza.

Eventually I managed to disentangle her sharp talons, push her back on her perch, and wedge it in the back.

"She didn't mean any harm," Humphrey said, mopping up blood from his neck. "It was only that we stopped suddenly and her perch was thrown forward. She just grabbed the nearest thing to steady herself."

I looked at Itza, and she looked solemnly back at me. We both knew better.

The rest of the journey passed off without incident, and we borrowed an empty hen house to instal Itza in.

"Don't let John go near her," we warned our host, as we saw his eldest son looking longingly at the hawks. "He can handle

Speckle if he likes, but this one is very cunning and dangerous."

Fortunately he stuck to our advice.

We had a lovely time at the Festival and on our return went to a wedding near Bridge of Earn. We parked our car for the reception in a field, with the windows slightly open so that the hawks would have enough air. It was a desperately hot day. Itza was in her usual place wedged into the back seat, and Speckle we had put on a block perch on the floor in front.

When we came back to the car Itza had somehow managed to upset her perch so that she was thrown forward, and a lightning steely claw had whipped out and killed poor Speckle. We were desolate. I refused to speak to Itza, and cried all the way home.

However a fortnight later we were to have a replacement for Speckle, a most beautiful huge female sparrowhawk, who came from Walter Joynson, and whom we christened Stella. Stella was delightful. She soon became just as tame as Speckle had been, and sat on my fingers. Adam was keen on handling her too, and had already learnt to do a very passable falconer's knot to tie her to her perch.

Adam was now far too big for Plum, and even Charlotte considered him a baby pony to ride. We knew that the essence of having Plum was not to be selfish over him, and after discussing it for some time, telephoned his original owner, Jean Rowan-Hamilton. Her son was just coming to the Plum-riding stage, and she made ready to welcome him home. He walked independently into the lorry which took him away, and drove off without a backward glance. It was, he felt, after all, au revoir and not goodbye. He was quite right. For several years to come, I met Plum socially at parties giving rides in the Rowan-Hamiltons' drawing room. He always knew me, and exchanged a gracious and kindly sniff.

At the same time we sold Crockett, who went for a children's pony to a man near Milnathort who thought him "a wee beauty". We did not agree, for although Crockett was an amusing colour, he had a very ugly head. We hoped Kitty was not going to miss him too much, but she was already wrapped up in Goldi-

166

locks and Kirsch. Kirsch was turning out a very handsome pony also, the same clear golden colour as Goldilocks, and both of them a little bigger than Kitty. It was sad to be so reduced in numbers, but we were hopeful of yet another pony arriving in the spring, for Kitty was in foal again.

We had now to consider finding homes for the basset puppies. We advertised them in the local paper, and had answers almost at once. We sold Kandy the same evening as the advertisement appeared to an elderly lady living in Dundee who wanted primarily a bed dog.

"He's not housetrained," we hastened to tell her, but she thought she would soon be able to cope with this one. She had brought a nice new lead and collar with her, and a special car rug to wrap him up in. We were very happy about his new home.

Kanute (whom we sometimes called Spot) went to a decorator also in Dundee, and grew into a huge and very ugly dog with a most savage bark. I once went to see him when he was quite grown up, but he did not recognize me at all. He still had the same spot on his tail.

Kentigern, one of the larger ones, went the next day to a keen hunting family in Angus. My mother fancied Kelinda for herself, and took her. She was a huge and a most beautiful hound, in appearance very like Grayling, who was after all her great-aunt.

So now feeling rather like the ten little nigger boys, we were left with five little basset hounds.

At the end of September we found in the farm steading an abandoned late hatch of swallows, two had fallen out of the broken nest and were dead, two were still alive. We tried catching flies and taking them down there, patching up the nest ourselves with mud, but we were not very successful, and the parents did not come back. Possibly they felt that it was too late in the year to rear a family and take them all that long way to the south. Realizing that the swallows were indeed abandoned, we brought them into the house, and made an imitation nest in our room. The winter was coming on and we found it desperately difficult to catch as many flies as we felt they must need. We found ourselves rather in the position of the picturesque peasants gathering wild flowers for that wretched Chocolat, except that collecting flies on other people's windows is not such a picturesque occupation.

We carried round a little match box each, and popped the dead flies into them. Part of the trouble was that we had to have such small flies—bluebottles were too big. The baby swallows flourished on our diet, and we could see their feathers growing longer and thicker, and their tails beginning to form. We had them for a week, and then one night they fell out of their nest in the kitchen were we had put them for additional warmth, and died. We were very sorry, although we had long known they could never have flown the distance, and we had worried about the eventual closing down of the fly supplies.

"But we could have popped them in a box, and given them to someone who was flying abroad, who could have released them." Some such plan had been at the back of our minds all the time, but now it was too late and they would never see the sun on the Pyramids, the bright bougainvillea, and the crisp scimitar shadows of the palm trees. We held the dead swallows in our hands and they were so light it was like holding the breath of the candle flame when it has blown into darkness. For us it was winter now and who knows if the same swallows will come back in the spring?

We agreed too that Stella should now be hacked back to the wild before it got too cold and difficult for her to go. We minded very much losing her, but how much better that she should go back to freedom and the wild wind torn branches in the autumn skies. It was difficult to remember not to speak to her, not to call her, or feed her on the fist, simply to leave the food for her to touch.

Soon she was bating off when we came into the Mews. She had regained her proper fear of us, and was ready for her freedom. We released her with a full crop, and she came back twice to her food lying waiting on the wall by the apple tree.

"There's one sparrowhawk you haven't been able to get," I said to Itza, who now was creeping closer and closer into the house, and had taken the goshawks' old perch in the kitchen.

We still had five bassets too many, so after some telephoning, we decided to send Kingly and Kinsman back to the Westerby, as being the biggest and most suitable for hunting. They were vast unhousetrained dogs, and I thought it might be nice to have them in our bed their last night, but it was not a success, and they had to be taken out comparatively early on. We took them to Perth Station holding them carefully on leads and collars, and they became great low dogs like badgers with no legs at all. One white, and one black, like vast hearthrugs they slunk along the platform. Then somehow they managed to slip out of their collars, and I was left holding the empty leads while they tore down the platform, upsetting people's luggage, barking wildly and wagging their tails. The whole station became pandemonium, Humphrey and I ran after them, and dived over barrows, caught a porter by the arm and spun him round as with a flying leap Humphrey managed to capture Kinsman. It was only with extreme reluctance that we got them tied up again and into the guard's van for their journey south.

"They'll obviously have a whale of a time in the pack," I commented. Their exuberance and joie de vivre was exciting and infectious.

The last three little bassets were much smaller. We advertised them again in the paper, and this time Keith went to someone in Errol, and Kindness, the little lemon and white bitch, to a woman who lived in Kirkcaldy. She had three children and a dachshund, but they had always wanted a basset hound as well. Kindness was wrapped in a rug they had brought for her, and put on the back seat between two of the children, who were already covering her with kisses when she went off.

Adam couldn't bear the hounds going, it made him very unhappy, and neither could Humphrey and I, though we felt it was in their best interest. We were left with little white Kestrel, the smallest and in some ways most endearing of the litter.

A Mr. Armstrong who worked in Perth telephoned. He said he was very anxious to have a basset hound, for they had just lost their Scottie whom they had for all the twelve years of their daughter's life, and she was heart-broken. I was doubtful if they would like a basset after a Scottie, both being such different breeds of dogs, with such differing temperaments. However I took Kestrel into Perth, and Mr. Armstrong fell in love with him at once, and carried him off there and then in a zip bag, with his little white head sticking out.

Some years later I learnt that Mr. Armstrong had left his job and become caretaker of a golf club, because it was a more suitable environment for Kestrel, and also that he had bought Keith to be a friend for his brother. If ever a basset fell firmly on his four paws it was Kestrel.

Itza continued to live in the kitchen, and sometimes would tuck her head right under her wing, which I suppose showed a certain confidence in us, but she never came to like us. I only had to get within inches of her, even when her head was tucked under her wing, for her to whip out her claw like lightning, and make a savage grab at me.

Humphrey tried several times to take her hawking, but although he got her trained to return to the fist, she would not fly, but came lolloping and lurching like a giant penguin. On one occasion he released her down hill at a rabbit in a field, thinking that she would have the advantage of the slope and might be able to glide down if nothing else. Having been thrown off the fist she had necessarily to plane down a short distance before she could land then instead of making for the rabbit, she turned straight round and began running back at Humphrey, and jumped at him striking his leg with her claw. It was only after this that Humphrey realized that her vicious temper was not inadvertent.

Another time, still trying to train her, they were out with Wond in the fields of the Carse below the house when Wond suddenly dived into the Pow and emerged with a large sea trout in her mouth—surely a unique thing for a pointer to do. Wond was very pleased with herself indeed.

In spite of not liking Itza, we had become accustomed to her, and were sorry that the climate of Scotland was so different from the sunshine in Peru. The weather depressed her, she developed worms, and died one afternoon sitting in the garage where we had put her to catch the last of the setting sun in a sheltered warmth. I felt like the Scottish minister who added, at the end of a long eulogy of a dead neighbour, "Mind you, I never liked the man."

But we missed having a hawk in the house, whatever she had been like, and so were glad when Susan Stirling asked if we would look after her peregrine Zita, while she was away. Zita was a dear beautiful bird, a true falcon with deep black eyes and creamy white and dark feathers. A peregrine is a true noble-man's hawk. To see her fly, speeding across the sky and then stooping like a thunderbolt to catch her prey with a swipe of her lightning talons, was to feel at one with the sky, to partake of another element. She was all air and fire and speed and bright-ness; to see her fluffed and cosy standing headless on one leg in our kitchen was to witness an almost unbelievable trans-formation.

There was one slight snag about taking Zita, and this was that we had promised to visit my parents who had taken a furnished house in the Isle of Man. However we presumed it was all right to take Zita with us as well. We went in February, and turned our van into a mobile hotel, spreading out a large foam rubber mattress across seats and suitcases in the back, with one reserved hawk corner where Zita would sit on her perch, and one kept for our bottled-gas ring and supplies of food. It was bitterly cold and slight snow on the ground, when we set out from home, hours later than we had meant to. We were to catch the 10 a.m. boat to the Isle of Man from Liverpool, and planned to drive down to Liverpool that day, spend the night there, and then catch the boat in comfort the next day. That was what we planned to do, but in reality, as so often seemed to happen to us, it was all very different.

There were last-minute things to see to, including explanations to Mrs. McAlpin about the feeding of the hens and Jemima and the pigeons, about hay for Kitty and Goldilocks and Kirsch, and extra oats for Kitty who was expecting a foal in the spring. There was far more packing than I had anticipated, things like the water to turn off, food to be packed in, including supplies for dogs and hawks. In the end it was nearly mid-day before we set off. We had a picnic lunch of soup and sandwiches in the car closely watched by Zita and the dogs, and then drove on through the rough snow covered roads and gathering darkness. TOM was so noisy that we simply had to stop now and then to rest our ears, but as soon as we stopped the temperature dropped right down. Adam and Charlotte were both warmly wrapped up, but even so the cold seeped through everything.

To make matters worse, there was something seriously wrong with TOM's engine. The noise got worse and worse, and we began to drive slower and slower.

The sun dropped red from the sky, and as darkness came on we fed Zita and the dogs, blessing our stove which enabled us to give them a hot dinner of meat and biscuit as well as making ourselves tea. We put even more clothes on the children, and bedded them down on the vast bed in the back. Then, gritting our teeth, we drove on through the whirling snowflakes. The engine got so bad that by the time we reached Carlisle at eleven o'clock we knew we should never make Shap unless we had some attention from a garage. It seemed only sense to try and mend it because being stuck on Shap in a blizzard in a broken-down van did not sound anyone's idea of fun.

We spent about an hour in the garage, and while Humphrey and the garage man were mending the engine, which was under the front seat, I had to get out, so I went and bought fish and chips, which were very refreshing and reviving. Adam and

Charlotte, who were half asleep woke up at the prospect of food, and so did the dogs, though Wond was choosy and only ate fish, but not chips.

Eventually the engine was sorted, and we started once more, at midnight.

"If we can only get over Shap, we'll be all right," I said.

"I believe it's very bad there," Humphrey said. "The chap in the garage said it was awful."

There is a long run up towards Shap. Tom did not take kindly to hills anyway, and with such a load was making heavy weather of it indeed. Also he had very small skiddy wheels which did not like snow, and whizzed and spun at every opportunity, The children, dogs and peregrine slept peacefully in the back, Adam and Charlotte tucked up warm beside the dogs, Zita sitting hunched on her perch. She thought it a poor exchange for her warm kitchen.

Peering into the driving snow we chugged slowly upwards. As the road got steeper, the surface got worse. At length when we got on to Shap itself we emerged into conditions so fantastic as to be unbelievable. The road was covered with packed snow, with here and there foot deep ruts worn in it by the wheels of heavy lorries into which our wheels plunged and lurched. It was like driving through a rough sea, with the difference that on one side there was a sheer drop down into the valley below. Over this appalling road bumped and thundered literally hundreds of giant lorries, all jolting and creaking at about five miles per hour. We knew that at that speed we would never make the summit, and would remain hopelessly stuck down below, perhaps to be bumped and pushed in our turn by the lorries until eventually thrown into the abyss.

So Humphrey put his foot down on the accelerator and made a run at it. It was the most horrifying drive I have ever known. To make matters worse he pressed his horn when passing one vast ninety-foot-long Leviathan and it stuck and blared concontinuously. We tried everything we could in desperation.

173

Lights flashed in our faces, horns were hooted back at us, and still the horn of TOM went stridently on.

"Do something about the horn!" Humphrey shouted above the noise.

"What can I do?" I shouted back.

"Cut it with something," Humphrey said, so pulling out the cords which attached the horn to the knob in the steering wheel I looked wildly in the back for something to cut it with. My eye fell on the picnic basket.

"Give me a knife, will you," I shouted to Adam who was awake, and he passed me the bread knife. A few determined saws, and the ghastly noise stopped.

Eventually we were over the summit and down the other side, and now the road steadily improved, until by the time we drove into Liverpool at four in the morning the snow had ceased to be anything more than a light powdering on the roofs of the houses. We parked in Exchange Square, and Humphrey and I, exhausted beyond anything, tumbled into the back beside Adam and Charlotte, Comfort and Wond, pulled the blankets and eiderdowns over us, and fell asleep.

When we woke up there was a large crowd of people standing pressed round the car peering in the windows at us. Zita peered back crossly, and moved on her perch preparing to bate off. I suppose a van full of sleeping people, dogs and children, not to mention a live peregrine, is rather an unusual thing to find in Exchange Square.

I left Humphrey to hold the fort and stick newspapers all round so as to protect Zita, while I took Charlotte into the station for a wash and brush up. We were in much need of it, and when we came back to let Humphrey and Adam go, found TOM well shrouded in newsprint, and the crowd, though still there, dispersing. Charlotte and I got the gas stove working, boiled up water for coffee, and cooked sausages and bacon. When Humphrey and Adam came back they found the crowd had grown if anything, all standing round and peering through the chinks in the newspaper to watch my cooking and wonder whether

Zita was alive or not. Eventually they dispersed and we had a cosy breakfast, brewing up a nice fug in the back of the car, and then drove down to the docks.

We left TOM in a car park, and proceeded to board the ferry, feeling rather like Mr. and Mrs. Noah preparing to embark. The officials seemed to think so too, for again a large crowd collected, and a worried man in a blue uniform with an official manner came bursting through to try and stop us taking Zita.

"You can't take hens to the Isle of Man because of fowl pest."

"But she's not a hen, she's a peregrine."

"Well, you can't take parrots because of psittacosis."

"But she's a peregrine falcon."

There was a pause, while he consulted his minutely printed instructions, but could find no reference anywhere to the importation of peregrines.

"Oh well," he said reluctantly, "Why didn't you say so in the first place?"

You can't win.

Our drive back was relatively unadventurous, and we called in at Keir on the way home and delivered Zita back to Susan. Our kitchen was once more hawkless. However Humphrey had been in correspondence with Colonel Lindquist, the Swedish falconer, and from him obtained a Lapland goshawk. She was a magnificent bird, bigger and more beautiful even than Hesse, and with the same warm responsive temperament. We called her Ragunda, and within a day or two she was living in the kitchen as if she had been there all her life.

At the beginning of April Susan Stirling telephoned. She said she had heard of two hawks in a pet shop in London which were in a very bad way, feathers broken, and looking exceptionally seedy. Would we consider rescuing them? One was a tawny eagle, she thought, the other some kind of a goshawk.

"I would take them myself, but I've already got a full mews. You may not be able to do much with them, but it would be a kindness to try."

Humphrey agreed to take them and they duly arrived at the station in the usual minute cardboard boxes. The goshawk was an African bird called a Chanting Goshawk. She was small with bright coral coloured legs, and soft grey feathers all over like a heron. We called her Coral because of her legs, but she was scary and not at all well. We brought her into the library, Ragunda having assumed command of the kitchen, and fed her carefully, but she had caught a severe chill and there was little we could do with her.

"She might pick up with a few nights in the warm," Humphrey said, but we were doubtful from the start. We could see that from a hawking point of view she was a useless bird, being no bigger than a small sparrowhawk, and with tiny thin legs like a buzzard which could catch and hold nothing bigger than a sparrow. She lived with us for a week, and Mr. Macrae came out to see her and said he did not think she would live that long.

Cronk, however, as we called the Tawny Eagle after the Manx word for a mountain, was a different matter. He was a young bird with broken feathers, not all full grown. A golden eagle is much harder penned than a tawny eagle, which has great soft feathers like an owl, and a gentle moth-like habit of flight. Cronk was about twice the size of Ragunda, but smaller than a golden eagle, and a darkish russety brown all over. He had much bigger legs and feet than a goshawk, and I noticed that Humphrey took care always to use a glove when dealing with Cronk. We had a special perch made for him, much bigger than a goshawk's, and he sat on this, and would fly to Humphrey on a long creance looking like a giant moth with soft lazy wing beats. Cronk had a huge eagle's beak which looked vicious, and until we were certain how he would react to us we treated him with due circumspection.

"After all," Humphrey said, "you can't afford to make a single mistake with an eagle."

For Adam's seventh birthday we had a Pirate Party, and flew the Jolly Roger from the top of Megginch—an ancient black-out curtain with skull and crossbones cut out from old sheets and tacked on by me. Both Cronk and Ragunda were there, though they took a non-active part, merely sitting on perches to add local colour as interesting Treasure Island fauna. We had an ingenious treasure map which showed where pirate's bootlaces and pipe were buried (liquorice of course) and also his glass eye (a marble), leading to the eventual discovery of an ancient iron chest full of gold bullion (chocolate, alas) which was on the top of a battlemented roof. Cronk and Ragunda watched with curious and unimpressed eyes.

May came, and with it a steam roller called Tiger, driven over by Humphrey and Vere Cochrane, an equally keen steam roller fan. They had arrived with no mishaps, apart from a slight contretemps with a fence which came away on their roller. Tiger was parked outside the Mews. The hens found it straight away, and the white hen made a nest in it, where she hatched out a large family of chickens. The dippers nested again by the waterfall, the grey wagtails came back to the wall, the swallows were all over our house, for our own six babies had come back in the spring, and Kitty gave birth to a fuzzy brown colt that we named Toffee.

Chapter 12

In June we gave Ragunda and Cronk to Walter Joynson, as we planned to take Adam and Charlotte in a sailing boat on the Dutch canals. Walter afterwards gave Cronk to John Murray, a keen eagle fan, who called him Lochinvar and made a great pet of him. Ragunda came home to Kilspindie to celebrate our return.

This year tragedy again struck the parent wagtails, but this time there were only eggs in the nest. Humphrey removed the eggs and, keeping them warm in his pocket, went ingeniously round several sparrows' nests, putting them in. It took rather a long time, because sometimes there were too many sparrows' eggs already there, and one had to be taken out, so that finally there were several sparrows' eggs to find nests for.

We left Wond and Comfort with my parents, and made arrangements about our other animals, and then flew off to Amsterdam, a very exciting trip for us, and especially for the children who were thrilled with the aeroplanes. We had, we discovered almost at once, made one mistake, and that was taking too much luggage. We had taken linen and various cooking utensils for the boat, and certain essential books which we had to cart with us, so that there were four heavy suitcases. They were too heavy for Adam and Charlotte to carry, so Humphrey and I had to struggle endlessly with two each.

We spent two nights in Amsterdam, and then went north to Friesland. Our boat was a small sailing one, with one cabin with two berths in it, and two minute berths in the fo'csle, in which Adam and Charlotte were to sleep. We took a taxi from the station to the boat hirer's yard, which was beside his house and simply a stretch of canal where several boats were tied up. We put our four terribly heavy suitcases on board, and then I suddenly realized that it was evening, and I had no food or provisions of any sort, there were no shops anywhere near, and once we got on to a boat it might be some time before we got near any.

The old man who was hiring the *Wetter Fugel* to us understood some English, and when I had explained my plight, he said, "Of course, you will take my wife's bicycle."

He showed me the direction the town lay in, and balancing two large shopping baskets on the handlebars I rode off on an early descendant of the penny-farthing. Sitting supremely erect, I pedalled along the dusty path beside the canal, looking and feeling rather ridiculous. Fortunately it was only two or three miles, and when I got to the town I found a market where I was able to get bread and butter, eggs and coffee and salad and cooked meat and fruit and milk, and even some vast packets of cornflakes. Balancing the whole precarious load on the bicycle I rode back, very slow and erect. I found Humphrey and the children had stowed all our kit on the boat, and he had been finding out how the engine worked, where the sails were, and how to put them all up and down. It was very hot still, and after I had returned the bicycle we boiled our kettle and made tea, which was very refreshing. Then we put up the sails, and taking advantage of the slight breeze, started off down the canal towards Leeuwarden, capital of Friesland.

There are Eleven Towns in Friesland, and in winter when it freezes, the great sport is to skate through them all on the same day, getting a card stamped at each one you go through. It took us rather longer to get through them all sailing, in fact a fortnight, but by the end we did it, and felt mildly triumphant.

The *Wetter Fugel* behaved beautifully, and we found she went equally well by sail or motor, though I preferred the motor, as I felt we had more control over the boat that way. Sometimes, as in Leeuwarden, we stayed in a grand Yacht Club harbour, but mostly we just tied up at the bank in the towns we came to, and Adam immediately climbed ashore with his fishing kit and joined all the little Dutch boys who were industriously fishing from the bank. He did catch two sad-looking fish once, which I cooked for him, but could not bring myself to eat them.

We found that in the greengrocer's they had vegetable washing and slicing machines which did all the vegetable cleaning for us, that in every shop, even the chemist's, the children were given sweets, and that all over Holland there are machines or stalls selling hot rissoles, sausages and chips, which are very good. We even found one woman who made them in her house, which we discovered by reading a neat little handwritten card stuck outside, and at half past nine at night she was quite ready to produce hot rissoles wrapped in paper for us all.

The nicest times were when we just tied up beside the bank of a canal, watching the white cloud processions sail by, across the endless expanse of blue sky, while black and white Friesian cows browsed and cropped the fields on either side. We thought we ought to hang a lantern at the end of the horizontal mast in case someone banged into us at night, so Adam, a reluctant volunteer in his pyjamas, sat on the mast and edged his way along the boat until he was able to hang the lantern on the back. In the morning he and Charlotte set off across the fields to the farmhouse where they somehow made the farmer understand their pidgin Dutch and were able to buy milk and eggs. They returned triumphant with them, and we had boiled new laid eggs for breakfast. Both children were in charge of the washing up, which they did in a plastic bowl on deck, and then threw the water overboard. One day they threw all our teaspoons overboard as well.

It was a time of complete enchantment. We tracked down steam organs, and found several, but the most magnificent one was G. Perlee's De Grouwe, all painted in pink and white and gold and drawn by two solid biscuit and white coloured horses called Connie and Nellie. We went into their stable where the children fed them with biscuits and helped to rub them down with a wisp of hay, and Humphrey turned the handle of the barrel organ. People came out into the street from their houses and began to dance, and Connie and Nellie (who were mother and daughter) snickered to each other, and accepted biscuits from us.

One day we went by train to Groningen where I launched a ship for some friends of ours. We started the day with an enormous lunch of chicken and ice cream, and then feeling so full we could hardly walk, drove to the docks. The *Saint Modan*, called after a Celtic saint, was to sail the western seas of Scotland trading among the islands. She looked perfectly enormous, and I felt suddenly nervous about the whole thing. However I grasped the champagne bottle firmly by its red-white-and-blue-ribboned neck and gave it a fair crack, and she positively exploded as she hit the ship. I felt that must be lucky.

Then the chocks were removed, and the ship moved slowly sideways to slip into the canal, causing a giant tidal wave which slopped up among the reeds on the other bank, and then came surging back again. One of the shipwrights gave me a lovely bouquet of golden pink roses tied with greeny gold ribbon and a beautiful silver dish full of scarlet and yellow gerberas. Then we all went into the office for an enormous tea, and when we had finished this, to Groningen for the most sumptuous banquet, course after course and wine after wine, and everyone drinking toasts, until late in the night, when we had to catch the last train back to Leeuwarden, with two sleepy and over-eaten children beside us. Humphrey carried Charlotte, but Adam, woken a little by the night air, walked back from the station to the yacht harbour, and across the narrow duck boards to where the *Wetter Fugel* was moored. It had been quite a day.

On we sailed through the canals, to a delightful mini-castle called the Popta Slot, and Franeker, with a handsome town hall, and a marvellous eighteenth-century Planetarium with a guide book in such ludicrous English that Humphrey offered to re-write it for them, and did, and they sent us a magnificent slab of chocolate with a picture of the Town Hall on it in white, and Christmas cards ever since.

We sailed to Harlingen, with its red lions standing heraldically on the bridge, and large harbours, and over for the day to the Island of Terschelling where the sands stretch out to the sky and meet at the world's end, and all is sea, and air and water, and there is nobody but the birds and the sands and the blue sky.

We left the *Wetter Fugel* tied up in Harlingen, and went for the day on the ordinary commercial boat, for we felt that it might only be courting disaster to sail into the North Sea by ourselves with the children. We knew about the North Sea. Going over on the boat the seagulls were so tame that they came down and took bread out of Adam's hands.

We went to Bolsward with its lovely carved church, and to Hindeloopen, a village rising out of the Zuider Zee, and populated by so many dogs, of pointer-like breeds, that we felt it might be difficult to be rid of them. They came and jumped into my lap when I sat for a moment sketching, and ran alongside the edge of the boat where Adam was trying to entice them on board. The sheep lay on the grass beside the boat munching, and the birds sailed past on the high wind out to the Zuider Zee. It looked choppy, and was, and both Charlotte and I felt very sea sick, and were. We were glad to make Staveren by nightfall.

We went to Sloten and Ijlst and across the wide Sneekermeer, and it was while we were sailing briskly down the canal just below it that we very nearly came to grief. We had all sails on and were sailing at a spanking pace, when we suddenly noticed a large concentration of boats lining the banks on both sides ahead of us.

"I wonder what all those boats are doing," I said casually to Humphrey.

He looked at them and then we both saw the huge swing railway bridge which was shut straight ahead of us. We had hardly time to haul down the sails, it looked as if we must smash into it and cut the mast in two. On we sped, faster and faster, through the two lines of anchored boats with everyone shouting, waving and pointing at us, and just as we got within ten yards of the railway bridge it began to lift, and had raised enough for us to squeeze through. It was a narrow thing.

Two days later we were saying goodbye to the *Wetter Fugel* and once more struggling with our suitcases in the Dutch railways. We went to Utrecht and Rotterdam, and then back home where we found Comfort had been hunting and had rolled in every imaginable filth and had to be given a thorough wash in the kitchen sink.

We went over to Walter and fetched Ragunda home, and it was as if we had never been away.

.   .   .

We had no central heating in our house but we had installed an oil stove in the front hall with a pipe which ran up through our clothes cupboard, and kept the entire house warm and dry. It was fed by a length of polythene tubing from a large tank in the garage. We had installed this after endlessly filling paraffin stoves, and lighting and cleaning fires. Twice the paraffin stove which we had put in our clothes cupboard had smoked and blackened all our clothes with oily soot so we were very pleased to have a more permanent arrangement.

One very cold night in early December Humphrey and I had just gone to bed and were discussing whether Ragunda should be brought in from the Mews or not. Suddenly I heard a curious hissing noise, and noticed that the room seemed to be getting rather dark.

I was just going to say to Humphrey, "I wonder if there's some water escaping somewhere?" when he said, "I think I'll go and have a look at the stove."

He went out then and a second or two later I heard him call up, "Cherry! Don't panic, just bring the small fire extinguisher from the bedroom mantelpiece."

Humphrey had spoken so calmly that naturally I didn't panic, but took the small fire extinguisher and went to the top of the stairs. It appeared to be pitch dark on the landing, and I could not imagine why Humphrey hadn't turned the light on. I

183

flicked the switch, but it made no difference. Suddenly I realized that it was dark because the entire house was black with smoke. I ran down the stairs to Humphrey in the front hall to give him the fire extinguisher and found the stove flaming with giant flames which shot up to the ceiling, the whole place suffocating and hot, and smoke in the back of my throat so that I coughed and coughed.

I remembered that there was another extinguisher in the kitchen, so groped my way along the back passage to get it. When I got back, it was too hot to breathe, and it seemed to me it would be only a matter of minutes before the whole house went up like a torch.

"I'd better get Adam and Charlotte out," I said to Humphrey, and he said, "Yes, you had."

It was only then I realized the seriousness of it all.

I stumbled back up the front stairs and into the children's bedroom, snatched Adam from the nearest bed and ran out with him, shutting the door behind me to prevent the smoke getting in to Charlotte. I couldn't carry them both at once. Holding Adam in my arms I cut quickly across the front landing, through the passage to the bathroom and down the back stairs to the back door at the bottom.

Adam half woke up as I dropped him down the last few stairs, shouting, "Get into the car outside," and ran back for Charlotte.

It was thicker than ever now, but no time to get anything to put over my face, so I put my hands over my mouth and nose, and ran coughing. It was still all right in the children's room, and Charlotte asleep, so I snatched her up, and ran out shutting the door, across the hot suffocating blackness, down the two steps, nearly tripping, and then through the passage and down the stairs and out.

I dared not think of Humphrey all this time, I only knew I must be as quick as possible. I ran out of the back door in my bare feet and nightdress, and thrust Charlotte into the car beside Adam, who I was glad to see had climbed into TOM.

The stars were brilliant, Northern lights flickering across

184

the far hill, and the ground shining with a myriad points of sparkling frost. I ran into the kitchen, snatched all the pile of assorted old coats which hang on the back of the door and thrust them into the car with the children, who were still clothed only in their nightdresses and pyjamas. "Wrap yourselves in these," I said as I hurled them through the door.

"The dogs," I thought desperately, "They were in our bedroom, and I didn't shut the door. The smoke will have got in there."

I knew I must get them out before trying to help Humphrey. Again I stumbled crossing the hot suffocating landing with the up and down steps, then I was along the passage and into our bedroom. Here the light was still on, but because I had left the door open the whole room was thick with smoke. I could not see at all. I called the dogs and walked forwards, feeling all over the bed with my hands, but they were not there. I banged against a small table on which was a tray of supper we had brought upstairs with us, and never eaten. The table and all the food upset with a crash on to the floor, and I found myself tripping over bits of brussels sprouts and broken plates.

"Wond! Comfort!" I called desperately. I began to go systematically over the room on all fours feeling with my hands. I could not find them anywhere. The bed was too low for them to get under. The smoke was very bad now, my eyes were streaming though I could see nothing, and I was coughing a lot.

"It's silly to go on looking, they can't be here," I thought. "If I stay any longer it will be too hot to get across that nasty bit of top landing."

I thought about the window if I couldn't get down through the house, but I didn't like it. It was all of twenty feet high, and stony underneath, and hardly fair on the baby who was due in three months' time.

"Wond! Comfort!" I called desperately. Surely they must hear me if they were here, or perhaps they were asphyxiated by the smoke as I felt myself becoming. I thought I had been systematically over all the room feeling, but somehow I had lost

185

my sense of direction and could not be sure that I had. I got up and went to the door, sure now they could not be there.

The smoke in the passage was worse. I could hear Humphrey coughing and choking down below, at least he was still alive, and I could hear the roaring of the flames. I wanted to shout to Humphrey to come out and leave it—it wasn't worth the risk. Somehow the danger, the horror of the situation reduced things very quickly to their real value. Humphrey and the children and the dogs mattered, and everything else was unimportant.

I staggered up to the back passage; surely the dogs must have followed me out when I went with the children. Both the doors of the children's room and the visitors' room were shut, and no one could have got down the front stairs. The back door stood wide open at the foot of the back stairs. I was sure now they had got out. After all, I knew they weren't in the bedroom; I had felt the bed, and every inch of the floor. I ran down the back stairs to see if I could see them outside and found a whole lot of oily rugs and towels blazing merrily on the gravel just under TOM's front wheels. If the car caught fire outside with the children in it that would be the last straw, I felt.

I jumped into the car, started the engine, and reversed backwards smartly, turned the car and drove down to the yard of the Manse opposite. I had a sudden horrid feeling that perhaps the whole house might be going to blow up, and that the further away the car was the safer it would be. Adam and Charlotte were still sleepy and a little alarmed. I told them to wrap up well in the coats, and stay in the car until we came for them, whatever happened. Then I jumped out, slammed the car door, and ran back up the road to Kilspindie.

The farm road was rough and stony to my bare feet, and the frost sparkling like a myriad diamonds on each sharp pointed stone made me feel like the little mermaid who walked on knives. My nightdress was short, and I had no dressing gown on, but I was running so hard I did not notice the cold. I tore back to the house, at least I could not see flames bursting through the roof, and found the front hall covered with black oil and water, and the fire quietly smouldering. Humphrey had got it out.

It was, I think, a miracle. I flew into his arms and we kissed each other.

"How did you do it?" I asked.

"Soaked towels in the bath and suffocated it," Humphrey said tersely. He looked at his watch. "Know what? It's only ten minutes since we were in bed first seeing that smoke."

It seemed unbelievable; a whole lifetime had passed in those ten minutes, it seemed another night, another year, since we were lying comfortably in bed. We opened all the windows and poured water on the smouldering remains. Everything was suddenly dank and cold. The clock in the front hall had melted, and so had the circle of iron hooks we hung the clothes on for airing; the wallpaper had gone, the paint was all scorched and blistered, and the whole place was covered with black oil.

"If we had telephoned for a fire engine, it couldn't have got here before twenty minutes from the time of telephoning," Humphrey said. "And it would have taken me two minutes to telephone, and in those two minutes the fire would have got too bad for me to have dealt with it. We would have lost everything."

Later we were glad of that too, but just then we were only able to share the relief that we were all well. I went back to the Manse to bring back the car with the children while Humphrey continued mopping up and putting out. I brought them upstairs to our bed and tucked them in. The window was wide open, and it was freezing cold.

"But what about the dogs?" Humphrey said. They were not in our bedroom. We could not find them anywhere.

"I expect they ran out of the back door, and have gone up the hill," I said.

Humphrey heated some soup, and brought up a half bottle of champagne. I cleared up the remains of our dinner; there was still quite a lot we could eat. Then I went along to the bathroom, and there, pitch black, sitting underneath the basin were

187

our own two dogs. They turned reproachful and furious eyes on me.

"Ha ha," they thought, "Fancy organizing something so awful and dreadful for us two poor dogs."

It was only with the greatest reluctance that they consented to be coaxed back to bed, where they lay sulkily, accepting tit-bits of food. We all sat in bed looking like coalmen, our faces were black, and the dogs were black all over, Humphrey's hands were burnt, my feet were cut and bleeding, and we all thanked God for bringing us that night safely out of the fire.

"It's funny," I said to Humphrey afterwards, "I always thought if there was a fire I should be terribly efficient. I would throw my jewellery out of the window, and save the photographs and some of the silver and one or two of the best bits of furniture, and some of my favourite clothes, and do you know, to-night, I never thought of any of those things at all. I just thought of you, and the babies, and the dogs."

"It's good for one sometimes," Humphrey said, "to be reminded of the things that really matter in the world."

After Christmas a new merlin came to us. We called her Pearly, and she was just as sweet as Morgan had been. She had to live in our bedroom because Ragunda had taken possession of the kitchen. At the end of February we all moved down to Megginch to stay with my parents, a huge caravan of us, for the arrival of our baby who was due early in March.

Here we slept in a room built in 1575, but the small oak four-poster bed was ninety years older, for Henry VII had slept in it on his way to the Battle of Bosworth Field. Pearly also slept on it, perched on the top corner like a small heraldic bird. Spring was coming, the blackbirds and thrushes already beginning to sing, the snowdrops and yellow frilled aconites like sheets of gold and silver in the woods, and in the Beech Walk the first double daffodils, planted more than a hundred years ago, were bursting into bloom. Chestnut buds were sticky, the elms covered in purple lace, and in less than six weeks the swallows would be with us.

Our new baby started to arrive at teatime on 11th March, and I told Charlotte when I put her to bed to pray for the baby to arrive that night. I knew about babies, and thought with any luck this one might be born about seven or eight in the morning, so I suggested Humphrey and my mother went to a cocktail party. My father and I sat waiting dinner for them, but by half past eight I realized that the baby was imminent, and asked my father to get Sister Walker.

Sister Walker came running upstairs. Somehow I got undressed and into bed, the doctor was telephoned for, Humphrey arrived back from the party at a quarter to nine, and at seven minutes past baby Humphrey came into the world crying loudly.

Sister Walker had a trying time, for Comfort, who was lying basset-o underneath the bed, chose the moment after Humphrey's birth to run out and lie cunningly on her feet, so she could hardly move at all. My mother came bursting in with the doctor a few minutes later, and I seemed to be drinking tea and champagne in alternate mouthfuls. Suddenly Sister Walker gave a little scream.

"It moved!" she said. "I swear it winked its eye at me."

"What did?" Humphrey asked.

"Your stuffed owl," she said.

Humphrey looked at Pearly who stood on one leg, pleasantly fluffed, looking inquiringly at the tiny red person who screamed in the cradle. "Oh you mean our merlin. She's tied up, but very much alive."

Later that night, as I lay too excited to sleep, I thought of all the babies who must have been born in that room, of all the babies who had lain breathing so quietly and softly in that cradle. It was a new life, something as frail and delicate as a candle flame, and yet as precious in the eyes of God as each new swallow, each fluffy white merlin. Pearly scratched her head lightly with her claw, and the bell tinkled delicately. Outside the grey light of dawn swept cold and clear across the marshes, and the geese flew past low from their midnight feeding grounds. Goose called to goose as they flew through the clear light of morning, and I thought of the cold dawn wind slicing through their pinion feathers. I wondered if our geese were flying with them high and free, and the new baby whimpered a little and slept, and the merlin slept, and I slept too, and the morning star came out in the green sky.